English Joy

조동인 저

도서출판
진영사

English Joy

조동인 저

2024년 12월 01일 초판 인쇄
2024년 12월 05일 초판 발행
발행인 박 진 영
발행처 도서출판 진영사
인천광역시 부평구 갈산동 주부토로 236 인천테크노밸리 U1 지식산업센터 B동 1507호
전화 : 032)505-4207
팩스 : 032)505-4206
E-mail : 0183734207@hanmail.net
신고번호 : 제2007-000001호

ISBN 978-89-6541-679-1 93740
값 18,000원

<CONTENTS>

English Joy

<CONTENTS>

<CONTENTS>

<CONTENTS>

<CONTENTS>

Chapter 1. Digital Communication

1 Dialogue Practice

Alex: Good morning, Jamie. Did you see the email from the project manager this morning?

Jamie: Good morning, Alex. Yes, I went through it. I think we need to discuss a few points in more detail.

Alex: I agree. The timeline seems a bit tight for the deliverables they're expecting.

Jamie: Exactly. I'm concerned about the quality if we rush it. Maybe we could negotiate a slight extension.

Alex: That's a good idea. Let's draft a response together. Should we address each point individually?

Jamie: Yes, that would be the best approach. We need to make our concerns clear without sounding defensive.

Alex: I'll start with the deadlines, and you can add points about the resource constraints.

Jamie: Perfect. I'll also mention the need for more team collaboration to handle this project effectively.

Alex: Great. Do you think we should loop in the team leads in this email?

Jamie: Definitely. Their input will strengthen our case for an extension.

Alex: What about the communication channels? Should we suggest a weekly check-in?

Jamie: That's an excellent idea. Regular updates will keep everyone aligned.

Alex: I'm glad we're on the same page. I'll also add a section about the expected outcomes to clarify our goals.

Jamie: Yes, that's crucial. Misunderstandings in digital communication can cause a lot of problems.

Alex: Speaking of which, did you see the new guidelines on video conferencing etiquette?

Jamie: I did. It's a good reminder to stay professional even if we're working remotely.

Alex: Agreed. Sometimes, the casual setting can make us forget we're still in a professional environment.

Jamie: So true. By the way, have you tried using the new project management tool they rolled out?

Alex: Yes, I've started using it. It's quite intuitive and helps keep everything organized.

Jamie: I've found it helpful too, especially for tracking tasks. I think it'll improve our efficiency.

Alex: Let's mention that in our email as well. It shows that we're proactive with the tools provided.

Jamie: Absolutely. It's essential to demonstrate that we're utilizing all resources available.

Alex: Do you think we should suggest any additional training on digital tools?

Jamie: That's a great idea. Some team members might not be as comfortable with them.

Alex: Good point. I'll include that in our proposal. Anything else we should cover?

Jamie: I think we've covered everything. Let's finalize it and send it over by the end of the day.

Alex: Sounds good. Thanks for collaborating on this, Jamie.

Jamie: No problem, Alex. Teamwork makes the dream work!

2 Sentence Practice

(1) The timeline seems a bit tight for the deliverables they're expecting.

(2) We need to make our concerns clear without sounding defensive.

(3) I'll also mention the need for more team collaboration.

(4) Regular updates will keep everyone aligned.

(5) Misunderstandings in digital communication can cause problems.

(6) The new guidelines on video conferencing etiquette are helpful.

(7) It's a reminder to stay professional in remote settings.

(8) The project management tool helps keep everything organized.

(9) Some team members might need training on digital tools.

(10) Teamwork makes the dream work!

3 Conversation Practice

1. What did Alex and Jamie discuss at the beginning of their conversation?
   (A) Project deadlines
   (B) An email from the project manager
   (C) A team meeting

2. What concern does Jamie have about the timeline?
   (A) It's too relaxed
   (B) It might compromise quality
   (C) It's unnecessary

3. How does Alex suggest they address their concerns in the email?
   (A) By addressing each point separately
   (B) By ignoring the manager's email
   (C) By calling a meeting

4. Who do Alex and Jamie want to include in the email?
   (A) The project manager only
   (B) The team leads
   (C) Their immediate supervisor

5. What does Alex suggest to improve communication on the project?
   (A) Weekly check-ins
   (B) Monthly updates
   (C) Daily reports

6. What does Jamie think about video conferencing etiquette?
   (A) It's unnecessary
   (B) It's a good reminder to stay professional
   (C) It's too strict

7. How does Jamie feel about the new project management tool?
   (A) It's difficult to use
   (B) It's helpful for tracking tasks
   (C) It's outdated

8. Why does Alex want to mention the project management tool in the email?
   (A) To show they're proactive
   (B) To complain about it
   (C) To avoid using it

9. What additional support does Jamie suggest for the team?
   (A) More time off
   (B) Training on digital tools
   (C) A larger budget

10. How does Alex describe digital communication misunderstandings?
   (A) They're common but harmless
   (B) They can cause problems
   (C) They're easy to avoid

11. What does Jamie mention about remote work?
(A) It's better than office work
(B) It's a reminder to stay professional
(C) It's very challenging

12. What does Alex plan to focus on in the email response?
(A) Deadlines
(B) Budgets
(C) Project cancellations

13. Why does Jamie support the idea of weekly check-ins?
(A) They will reduce misunderstandings
(B) They're unnecessary
(C) They replace individual emails

14. What is the purpose of the email Alex and Jamie are drafting?
(A) To request a deadline extension
(B) To suggest a new project
(C) To resign from their roles

15. What suggestion does Alex make about digital tool training?
(A) It's not needed
(B) Some team members might benefit from it
(C) It's too expensive

16. How does Jamie describe the new project management tool?
   (A) Intuitive
   (B) Difficult
   (C) Outdated

17. What phrase does Jamie use to emphasize teamwork?
   (A) "Communication is key!"
   (B) "Teamwork makes the dream work!"
   (C) "Working together is better!"

18. How do Alex and Jamie feel about using digital communication tools?
   (A) They're skeptical
   (B) They see them as helpful
   (C) They avoid them

19. What kind of attitude does Jamie want to avoid in the email?
   (A) Defensive
   (B) Supportive
   (C) Enthusiastic

20. What does Alex suggest adding to clarify their goals?
   (A) An appendix
   (B) A section on expected outcomes
   (C) Personal opinions

21. How does Jamie feel about professional development on digital tools?
   (A) It's unnecessary
   (B) It's beneficial
   (C) It's too expensive

22. What is the overall tone of the conversation?
   (A) Casual
   (B) Professional
   (C) Hostile

23. What concern does Alex have about rushing the project?
   (A) It will look unprofessional
   (B) It may compromise quality
   (C) It will exceed the budget

24. What does Jamie suggest regarding team collaboration?
   (A) It's not necessary
   (B) It's crucial for success
   (C) It's an extra effort

25. How does Alex plan to address project constraints?
   (A) By ignoring them
   (B) By discussing them in the email
   (C) By requesting additional resources

26. Why is regular communication important according to Jamie?
   (A) It saves time
   (B) It prevents misunderstandings
   (C) It eliminates all problems

27. What is Alex's view on remote work etiquette?
   (A) It's unnecessary
   (B) It's essential
   (C) It's outdated

28. What does Jamie think of the project management tool's efficiency?
   (A) It's slow
   (B) It's very efficient
   (C) It needs improvement

29. What does Alex prioritize when managing tight deadlines?
   (A) Flexibility
   (B) Efficiency
   (C) Quality

30. How do both feel about utilizing digital resources?
   (A) They find it essential
   (B) They're indifferent
   (C) They dislike it

〈Conversation Practice Answer Key〉

(1) (B)
(2) (B)
(3) (A)
(4) (B)
(5) (A)
(6) (B)
(7) (B)
(8) (A)
(9) (B)
(10) (B)
(11) (B)
(12) (A)
(13) (A)
(14) (A)
(15) (B)
(16) (A)
(17) (B)
(18) (B)
(19) (A)
(20) (B)
(21) (B)
(22) (B)
(23) (B)
(24) (B)
(25) (B)
(26) (B)
(27) (B)
(28) (B)
(29) (C)
(30) (A)

4 Paragraph Practice

Questions 1–4 refer to the following paragraph.

Jessica recently started using a new digital communication tool to streamline her workflow. She finds the 1. _______ very user-friendly, which makes managing tasks easier. However, she has noticed that some of her team members are 2. _______ in adopting the new tool. To address this, she arranged a training session to make sure everyone understands its features. Jessica believes that with consistent practice, her team will 3. _______ the tool effectively and increase productivity. Overall, she feels optimistic about the tool's potential to improve their 4. _______ communication.

1.

(A) design (B) support

(C) cost (D) interface

2.

(A) reluctant (B) eager

(C) aggressive (D) excited

3.

(A) abandon (B) master

(C) ignore (D) delete

4.

(A) face-to-face (B) sporadic

(C) digital (D) physical

〈Paragraph Practice Answer Key〉

(1) (D)

(2) (A)

(3) (B)

(4) (C)

5 Idiom Practice

1. Ping someone – To send a quick message or notification.
   "I'll ping you the details once the meeting starts."

2. Hit the ground running – To begin a task with full energy and efficiency.
   "The new manager hit the ground running with the latest project."

3. In the loop – To be kept informed about the latest updates.
   "Please keep me in the loop about any developments."

4. Bandwidth – The mental or physical capacity to take on tasks.
   "I don't have the bandwidth to take on more projects right now."

5. Circle back – To revisit a topic later.
   "Let's circle back to this point after we address other issues."

6. On the same page – To have mutual understanding in communication.
   "It's important for the team to be on the same page."

7. Touch base – To briefly connect or follow up.
   "I'll touch base with you tomorrow to finalize the details."

8. Off the grid – To be disconnected from digital communication.
   "He went off the grid during his vacation."

9. Red flag – A warning sign.
   "His lack of response to emails was a red flag."

10. Up to speed – Being fully informed or knowledgeable.
    "I'll bring you up to speed on the project during our call."

Chapter 2. Public Speaking and Presentation

1 Dialogue Practice

Emma: Hi, Daniel! I heard you're preparing for a big presentation. How's it going?

Daniel: Hi, Emma! Yes, it's for our annual conference. It's been a challenging process, but I'm making progress.

Emma: That sounds exciting but also nerve-wracking. What's the main topic of your presentation?

Daniel: It's about the impact of digital transformation on our industry. I want to convey how it affects both businesses and consumers.

Emma: That's a great topic. Are you focusing on any particular aspect?

Daniel: Yes, I'm highlighting the role of artificial intelligence and automation. It's fascinating but a bit complex.

Emma: True, explaining complex topics in a simple way can be tricky. How are you structuring your presentation?

Daniel: I'm starting with an overview, followed by case studies, and ending with future predictions.

Emma: Sounds logical. Are you using any visuals to support your points?

Daniel: Definitely. I have charts, graphs, and a few short videos. Visuals make it easier for the audience to grasp the information.

Emma: Absolutely. What about your opening? It's crucial to grab their attention right from the start.

Daniel: I'm starting with a surprising statistic. I think it'll capture their interest immediately.

Emma: Smart move! And for your conclusion?

Daniel: I'm summarizing the key points and ending with a call to action, encouraging everyone to embrace digital tools.

Emma: Perfect. Have you practiced in front of a small audience yet?

Daniel: Yes, I practiced with some colleagues, and they gave me valuable feedback.

Emma: That's helpful. Did they suggest any improvements?

Daniel: They mentioned I should speak a bit slower and make eye contact more often. It's easy to get carried away when presenting.

Emma: Very true. Maintaining a steady pace and eye contact can make a big difference.

Daniel: I'm working on it. I'm also trying to eliminate filler words like "um" and "you know."

Emma: Those are tough to avoid, but practice makes perfect. Do you get nervous before speaking?

Daniel: I do, but I try to channel the nervous energy into enthusiasm. It helps me connect with the audience.

Emma: That's a great approach. Are you using any specific techniques to calm your nerves?

Daniel: Yes, deep breathing exercises and visualization. They help me stay calm and focused.

Emma: That's excellent. What about the Q&A session? Are you prepared for questions?

Daniel: I am. I've anticipated some potential questions and prepared answers in advance.

Emma: Good idea. How do you handle questions you don't know the answer to?

Daniel: I'll be honest and admit I'll need to research it further. Honesty builds credibility.

Emma: Absolutely. Have you timed your presentation to ensure it fits the allocated time?

Daniel: Yes, I'm aiming for 20 minutes, leaving 10 minutes for questions. Time management is essential.

Emma: You're well-prepared, Daniel. I'm sure your presentation will be a success!

Daniel: Thank you, Emma. Your feedback has been incredibly helpful.

2 Sentence Practice

(1) I'm starting with a surprising statistic to capture their interest immediately.

(2) I'm highlighting the role of artificial intelligence and automation.

(3) Visuals make it easier for the audience to grasp the information.

(4) I'm summarizing the key points and ending with a call to action.

(5) Practicing with colleagues can provide valuable feedback.

(6) Maintaining a steady pace and eye contact can make a big difference.

(7) Deep breathing exercises and visualization help me stay calm.

(8) I've prepared answers for potential questions in advance.

(9) Honesty builds credibility during Q&A sessions.

(10) Time management is essential to fit within the allocated time.

3 Conversation Practice

1. What is Daniel preparing for?
   (A) A job interview
   (B) A big presentation
   (C) A team meeting

2. What is the main topic of Daniel's presentation?
   (A) Artificial intelligence
   (B) Digital transformation
   (C) Marketing strategies

3. How is Daniel structuring his presentation?
   (A) Overview, case studies, future predictions
   (B) Introduction, body, conclusion
   (C) Only a Q&A session

4. What does Daniel plan to use to support his points?
   (A) Text-based slides only
   (B) Charts, graphs, and videos
   (C) Handouts

5. How does Daniel plan to start his presentation?
   (A) With a joke
   (B) With a surprising statistic
   (C) By introducing himself

6. What will Daniel conclude his presentation with?
   (A) A joke
   (B) A call to action
   (C) A summary of his personal achievements

7. Who gave Daniel feedback after his practice?
   (A) His family
   (B) His colleagues
   (C) His manager

8. What was one of the suggestions his colleagues gave?
   (A) To speak faster
   (B) To use more filler words
   (C) To make more eye contact

9. What technique does Daniel use to calm his nerves?
   (A) Ignoring the audience
   (B) Deep breathing exercises
   (C) Rushing through the presentation

10. How does Daniel handle questions he doesn't know the answer to?
   (A) By guessing
   (B) By being honest
   (C) By avoiding the question

11. What does Daniel aim for in terms of timing?
    (A) 30 minutes for speaking
    (B) 20 minutes for speaking and 10 for Q&A
    (C) Only 5 minutes of speaking

12. What does Emma suggest to grab the audience's attention?
    (A) Use humor
    (B) Use a powerful statistic
    (C) Skip the introduction

13. How does Daniel describe filler words?
    (A) Helpful
    (B) Hard to avoid
    (C) Necessary

14. What role does Daniel believe eye contact plays?
    (A) It makes him uncomfortable
    (B) It helps connect with the audience
    (C) It's not important

15. How does Daniel plan to handle his nervous energy?
    (A) By ignoring it
    (B) By channeling it into enthusiasm
    (C) By stopping mid-presentation

16. What is Daniel's main focus during his conclusion?
   (A) To end abruptly
   (B) To encourage the audience to embrace digital tools
   (C) To repeat his entire presentation

17. What is Daniel's attitude towards Q&A sessions?
   (A) He avoids them
   (B) He feels prepared
   (C) He dislikes them

18. What does Daniel believe about admitting he doesn't know an answer?
   (A) It makes him look unprepared
   (B) It builds credibility
   (C) It's unnecessary

19. What is Emma's advice on nervousness?
   (A) Ignore it completely
   (B) Channel it into enthusiasm
   (C) Skip the presentation

20. What kind of visuals does Daniel plan to use?
   (A) Only text
   (B) Interactive models
   (C) Charts and graphs

21. Who suggests adding a section on expected outcomes?
   (A) Emma
   (B) Daniel
   (C) The project manager

22. How does Daniel keep track of time during practice?
   (A) By setting a timer
   (B) By guessing
   (C) By asking Emma

23. How does Daniel feel about using visuals?
   (A) They're distracting
   (B) They enhance understanding
   (C) They're unnecessary

24. What was Emma's role in helping Daniel?
   (A) She gave feedback and advice
   (B) She critiqued his presentation harshly
   (C) She ignored his questions

25. How does Daniel describe the importance of the introduction?
   (A) It's not important
   (B) It grabs the audience's attention
   (C) It's better to skip

26. Why does Daniel want to add a call to action?
    (A) To end on a strong note
    (B) To make people laugh
    (C) To confuse the audience

27. How does Daniel handle his pace during the presentation?
    (A) By speaking fast
    (B) By maintaining a steady pace
    (C) By rushing

28. What does Daniel say about practice?
    (A) It's unnecessary
    (B) It's key to improvement
    (C) It makes him nervous

29. What type of exercise does Daniel use to calm down?
    (A) Walking around the room
    (B) Deep breathing
    (C) Speaking loudly

30. How does Daniel plan to engage with the audience?
    (A) By ignoring their questions
    (B) By making eye contact
    (C) By reading from a script

〈Conversation Practice Answer Key〉

(1) (B)
(2) (B)
(3) (A)
(4) (B)
(5) (B)
(6) (B)
(7) (B)
(8) (C)
(9) (B)
(10) (B)
(11) (B)
(12) (B)
(13) (B)
(14) (B)
(15) (B)
(16) (B)
(17) (B)
(18) (B)
(19) (B)
(20) (C)
(21) (B)
(22) (A)
(23) (B)
(24) (A)
(25) (B)
(26) (A)
(27) (B)
(28) (B)
(29) (B)
(30) (B)

4 Paragraph Practice

Questions 1-4 refer to the following paragraph.

Megan was scheduled to present a project proposal to the executive team. She prepared a detailed slideshow with graphs and statistics to 1. _______ her arguments. Megan practiced multiple times, ensuring that she could stay within the allotted time and answer any questions confidently. On the day of the presentation, she took a deep breath, reminded herself of her 2. _______ points, and began speaking clearly. Although a few questions were challenging, she handled them with 3. _______ and finished on a strong note. After the presentation, she felt 4. _______ about her performance and was eager to hear the feedback.

1.

(A) confuse　　(B) highlight

(C) oppose　　(D) simplify

2.

(A) minor　　(B) main

(C) confusing　　(D) last

3.

(A) hesitation　　(B) confidence

(C) confusion　　(D) insecurity

4.

(A) disappointed　　(B) uncertain

(C) positive　　(D) nervous

〈Paragraph Practice Answer Key〉

(1) (B)

(2) (B)

(3) (B)

(4) (C)

5 Idiom Practice

1. Break the ice – To start a conversation in a way that makes people feel more comfortable.
   "He used a joke to break the ice at the beginning of his presentation."

2. Steal the show – To be the most outstanding in a performance or event.
   "Her presentation stole the show at the conference."

3. On the same wavelength – To have a mutual understanding with someone.
   "It's crucial to be on the same wavelength as your audience."

4. Put the spotlight on – To focus attention on something.
   "He put the spotlight on key statistics to support his argument."

5. Smooth sailing – To proceed without any problems.
   "After the introduction, the rest of the presentation was smooth sailing."

6. In the limelight – To be the center of attention.
   "He didn't expect to be in the limelight during the Q&A session."

7. Catch their attention – To grab the audience's interest.
   "He started with a shocking fact to catch their attention."

8. A hard act to follow – Someone or something that is difficult to surpass.
   "His presentation was so good, it's going to be a hard act to follow."

9. Off the cuff – To speak without preparation.
   "She answered the questions off the cuff and impressed the team."

10. Get the ball rolling – To start something.
    "She decided to get the ball rolling by introducing a bold idea."

Chapter 3. Giving and Following Instructions

1 Dialogue Practice

Sarah: Hi, Tom! Can you explain the new filing system to me?

Tom: Of course, Sarah. First, we organize all files by project, then by client within each project.

Sarah: Got it. Do I start by labeling each folder with the project name?

Tom: Exactly. Once labeled, each project folder goes into the main directory.

Sarah: And within each project folder, do I categorize by client files?

Tom: Yes, that's right. Place all client files under the respective project.

Sarah: Understood. What should I do if a client has multiple projects?

Tom: In that case, create a separate project folder for each one and label them clearly.

Sarah: That makes sense. Where do I put completed project files?

Tom: Move completed projects to the "Archived" folder. It keeps things tidy.

Sarah: Okay. How often should I archive completed files?

Tom: We usually archive at the end of each month, but you can do it as needed.

Sarah: What if I need to retrieve an archived file later?

Tom: All archived files are organized the same way, so finding them should be straightforward.

Sarah: Should I inform anyone before archiving?

Tom: Yes, please notify your supervisor to confirm all files are complete.

Sarah: Understood. And for the digital files, do I follow the same structure?

Tom: Absolutely. The structure remains consistent across both physical and digital files.

Sarah: Should I back up digital files too?

Tom: Yes, we back up everything weekly to prevent data loss.

Sarah: That's a good precaution. Who's responsible for the backups?

Tom: IT manages the backups, but it's good to check that your files are included.

Sarah: Got it. How do I handle duplicate files?

Tom: Delete any unnecessary duplicates, but keep any needed for cross-referencing.

Sarah: Thanks, Tom. How do I identify files needing cross-referencing?

Tom: Usually, files used by multiple departments require cross-referencing.

Sarah: And I assume those files should stay in the active directory?

Tom: Correct. Don't archive them unless they're no longer needed by all departments.

Sarah: Should I create any specific notes for these files?

Tom: Adding a "cross-reference" tag to the folder will be helpful for others.

Sarah: That's a great tip. Anything else I should be aware of?

Tom: Just remember to review the directory weekly for any updates or changes.

Sarah: Will do. How do I handle client requests for old files?

Tom: Retrieve them from the archive, but make a copy and keep the original archived.

Sarah: What about sensitive files? Is there a different process?

Tom: Sensitive files go into the "Confidential" folder and are password-protected.

Sarah: Makes sense. Who sets the password?

Tom: The supervisor will assign a password and provide it to authorized personnel.

Sarah: And for files we're required to keep permanently?

Tom: Label those as “Permanent Record” and store them separately from regular files.

Sarah: How often should I review permanent records?

Tom: Annually is usually sufficient, but check with your supervisor.

Sarah: I think I have everything now. Thanks for your patience, Tom.

Tom: No problem, Sarah. You'll get the hang of it in no time!

2 Sentence Practice

(1) Organize all files by project, then by client within each project.

(2) Place completed projects in the "Archived" folder at the end of each month.

(3) Archived files are organized the same way as active files for easy retrieval.

(4) Notify your supervisor before archiving any completed files.

(5) Follow the same structure for both physical and digital files.

(6) Back up digital files weekly to prevent data loss.

(7) Delete unnecessary duplicate files unless needed for cross-referencing.

(8) Files used by multiple departments may need cross-referencing.

(9) Add a “cross-reference” tag to help others identify shared files.

(10) Store permanent records separately and review them annually.

3 Conversation Practice

1. How are the files organized first?
   (A) By client
   (B) By project
   (C) By date

2. Where should completed projects be stored?
   (A) In the main directory
   (B) In the "Archived" folder
   (C) In a separate directory

3. How often should files be archived?
   (A) Weekly
   (B) Monthly
   (C) Daily

4. What is the procedure if a client has multiple projects?
   (A) Put all projects in one folder
   (B) Create separate project folders
   (C) Ignore extra projects

5. How are archived files organized?
   (A) Randomly
   (B) The same way as active files
   (C) By date only

6. Who should be informed before archiving files?
   (A) The supervisor
   (B) The IT department
   (C) The client

7. Should digital files follow the same structure?
   (A) No, they have a different structure
   (B) Yes, they follow the same structure
   (C) Only for sensitive files

8. How often are digital files backed up?
   (A) Weekly
   (B) Monthly
   (C) Annually

9. Who manages the file backups?
   (A) Each department
   (B) IT
   (C) The supervisor

10. What should be done with duplicate files?
   (A) Delete them
   (B) Store them separately
   (C) Keep them if needed for cross-referencing

11. How should cross-referenced files be tagged?
   (A) As "Duplicate"
   (B) As "Cross-reference"
   (C) As "Confidential"

12. Where should sensitive files be stored?
   (A) In the "Archived" folder
   (B) In the "Confidential" folder
   (C) In the "Client" folder

13. Who sets the password for sensitive files?
   (A) The IT team
   (B) The supervisor
   (C) The employee

14. How should permanent records be labeled?
   (A) As "Archived"
   (B) As "Permanent Record"
   (C) As "Confidential"

15. How often should permanent records be reviewed?
   (A) Monthly
   (B) Weekly
   (C) Annually

16. What should be done when retrieving old files for clients?
   (A) Take the original file out of the archive
   (B) Make a copy and leave the original in the archive
   (C) Inform the client to get it themselves

17. Where do files used by multiple departments go?
   (A) In the "Confidential" folder
   (B) In the active directory
   (C) In the "Archived" folder

18. Who should authorize archiving sensitive files?
   (A) The supervisor
   (B) The client
   (C) IT

19. How often should the directory be reviewed for updates?
   (A) Monthly
   (B) Weekly
   (C) Quarterly

20. Who handles file tagging for cross-referencing?
   (A) IT
   (B) The employee managing the files
   (C) The supervisor

21. What is the purpose of labeling permanent records?
   (A) To discard them easily
   (B) To store them separately
   (C) To reuse them later

22. How should one handle a client's request for old files?
   (A) Send the original file
   (B) Create a copy
   (C) Store it in the "Archived" folder

23. What should be done with unnecessary duplicate files?
   (A) Archive them
   (B) Delete them
   (C) Keep them for reference

24. Who is responsible for the weekly backup of digital files?
   (A) IT
   (B) Each employee
   (C) The supervisor

25. Where should client files be placed?
   (A) Within each project folder
   (B) In a separate directory
   (C) Under the "Confidential" folder

26. How do you handle files needing cross-referencing?
   (A) Move them to the "Archived" folder
   (B) Tag them and keep in the active directory
   (C) Delete them if not needed

27. What's the first step in organizing the new filing system?
   (A) Label each folder with the project name
   (B) Inform the supervisor
   (C) Create duplicate files

28. What should you do if the files are needed for multiple departments?
   (A) Archive them
   (B) Cross-reference them
   (C) Discard them

29. Who should verify files before archiving?
   (A) The client
   (B) The employee
   (C) The supervisor

30. What should be the last step before archiving?
   (A) Notify the client
   (B) Label as "Archived"
   (C) Review with the supervisor

〈Conversation Practice Answer Key〉

(1) (B)
(2) (B)
(3) (B)
(4) (B)
(5) (B)
(6) (A)
(7) (B)
(8) (A)
(9) (B)
(10) (C)
(11) (B)
(12) (B)
(13) (B)
(14) (B)
(15) (C)
(16) (B)
(17) (B)
(18) (A)
(19) (B)
(20) (B)
(21) (B)
(22) (B)
(23) (B)
(24) (A)
(25) (A)
(26) (B)
(27) (A)
(28) (B)
(29) (C)
(30) (C)

4 Paragraph Practice

Questions 1–4 refer to the following paragraph.

Kelly was tasked with creating a guide for new employees on how to follow the office protocols. She 1. ______ each section to make the guide easy to understand, covering important areas such as dress code, communication etiquette, and use of office resources. After drafting each section, she 2. ______ with team leaders to ensure accuracy. Kelly included a special note about the protocol for securing confidential information and emphasized the importance of 3. ______ passwords regularly. Once finished, she distributed the guide to the department heads, who would then 4. ______ it with their teams.

1.
(A) categorized (B) ignored
(C) complicated (D) clarified

2.
(A) bypassed (B) consulted
(C) excluded (D) replaced

3.
(A) deleting (B) remembering
(C) updating (D) simplifying

4.
(A) review (B) discard
(C) update (D) overlook

〈Paragraph Practice Answer Key〉

(1) (A)

(2) (B)

(3) (C)

(4) (A)

5 Idiom Practice

1. Follow suit – To do the same thing as someone else.
   "After seeing the success of the new filing system, other departments decided to follow suit."

2. Show someone the ropes – To teach someone how to do a particular job.
   "He showed the new intern the ropes on using the company's database."

3. In black and white – Clearly written or stated.
   "The company policy was laid out in black and white."

4. Go by the book – To follow rules strictly.
   "They insist that everyone goes by the book when handling sensitive files."

5. Get the ball rolling – To start something.
   "He got the ball rolling on the new filing system."

6. Leave no stone unturned – To search or examine thoroughly.
   "She left no stone unturned while organizing the files."

7. Step up to the plate – To take responsibility for something.
   "He stepped up to the plate when his team needed help with archiving."

8. Learn the ropes – To understand how things work in a particular situation.
   "It took her a week to learn the ropes of the new system."

9. Take it step by step – To do something gradually or carefully.
   "She took it step by step when explaining the process to the new hire."

10. By the book – Following the rules exactly.
    "He handled the document transfer strictly by the book."

Chapter 4. Problem Solving and Decision Making

1 Dialogue Practice

Alice: Hi, Ben. I heard you're facing some challenges with the project timeline.
Ben: Hi, Alice. Yes, we're a bit behind schedule, and I'm struggling to prioritize tasks effectively.

Alice: Have you considered breaking down the project into smaller, manageable parts?
Ben: That's a good idea. I often feel overwhelmed by the scope of the project.

Alice: It might help to focus on one phase at a time. Also, have you tried delegating tasks?
Ben: Not as much as I should. I tend to take on too much myself.

Alice: Delegation can be really beneficial. It allows you to leverage the strengths of your team members.
Ben: You're right. I'll start assigning tasks more strategically.

Alice: Another tip is to set milestones. It keeps everyone on track and motivated.
Ben: I like that. Small wins can make a big difference.

Alice: Exactly. Have you identified the biggest challenges yet?
Ben: Yes, mainly resource allocation and meeting the client's changing requirements.

Alice: Perhaps you could schedule regular check-ins with the client to manage expectations.

Ben: That's smart. It would also help in addressing any scope changes early on.

Alice: Also, don't hesitate to communicate any delays. Transparency builds trust.

Ben: I agree. I think I've been avoiding those conversations to avoid disappointment.

Alice: Most clients appreciate honesty. It's better than surprising them last minute.

Ben: True. I'll work on keeping them updated more consistently.

Alice: Have you tried using any project management tools?

Ben: I'm using a basic one, but maybe upgrading could help with tracking.

Alice: There are plenty of advanced tools that provide real-time updates and visual timelines.

Ben: I'll look into that. Any specific tool you'd recommend?

Alice: Trello and Asana are quite popular and user-friendly.

Ben: Great, I'll give those a try. What about managing my team's workload?

Alice: Perhaps you could implement a rotating schedule to balance tasks.

Ben: I hadn't thought of that. It could prevent burnout.

Alice: Absolutely. And it fosters a sense of shared responsibility.

Ben: Thanks for all the advice, Alice. You've given me a lot to think about.

Alice: Anytime, Ben. Remember, problem-solving is a skill that improves with practice.

Ben: I'll keep that in mind. I feel more confident already.

Alice: Glad to hear it! Let me know if you need any more help.

Ben: I definitely will. Thanks again for your time.

Alice: No problem. Let's make this project a success together!

2 Sentence Practice

(1) Breaking down a project into manageable parts can reduce overwhelm.

(2) Setting milestones keeps the team motivated and on track.

(3) Delegating tasks allows you to leverage team strengths.

(4) Regular check-ins with clients help manage expectations effectively.

(5) Transparent communication builds trust with clients.

(6) Project management tools offer real-time updates and tracking features.

(7) Implementing a rotating schedule can prevent team burnout.

(8) Addressing scope changes early avoids last-minute issues.

(9) Problem-solving is a skill that improves with practice.

(10) Celebrating small wins boosts morale during challenging projects.

3 Conversation Practice

1. What is Ben struggling with in his project?
   (A) Delegating tasks
   (B) Prioritizing tasks
   (C) Meeting clients

2. What does Alice suggest to manage the project better?
   (A) Outsource the work
   (B) Divide the project into parts
   (C) Finish the project early

3. How does Ben usually handle tasks?
   (A) He delegates most tasks
   (B) He takes on too much himself
   (C) He avoids challenging tasks

4. What does Alice recommend for keeping the team motivated?
   (A) Offering bonuses
   (B) Setting milestones
   (C) Working longer hours

5. What is Ben's main challenge with the client?
   (A) Lack of communication
   (B) Changing requirements
   (C) Insufficient budget

6. Why does Alice suggest regular check-ins with the client?
   (A) To avoid scope changes
   (B) To manage expectations
   (C) To complete the project faster

7. How does Ben feel about being honest with clients?
   (A) He avoids it
   (B) He finds it easy
   (C) He doesn't think it's necessary

8. What is Ben using to manage his project?
   (A) Trello
   (B) A basic project management tool
   (C) Asana

9. Which project management tool does Alice recommend?
   (A) Slack
   (B) Asana
   (C) Google Drive

10. Why does Alice suggest a rotating schedule?
   (A) To increase workload
   (B) To balance tasks and prevent burnout
   (C) To reduce overall project time

11. What does Alice believe about problem-solving?
    (A) It's an innate skill
    (B) It improves with practice
    (C) It should be avoided

12. How does Ben feel after talking with Alice?
    (A) Confident
    (B) Confused
    (C) Overwhelmed

13. How does Alice suggest Ben handle scope changes?
    (A) Ignore them
    (B) Address them early
    (C) Ask the client to change them

14. What does Alice say about clients and honesty?
    (A) They don't care about transparency
    (B) They appreciate honesty
    (C) They only want positive updates

15. What's one way to track team progress that Alice suggests?
    (A) Weekly meetings
    (B) Celebrating big wins
    (C) Using project management tools

16. What does Ben plan to do regarding project tracking tools?
   (A) Ignore Alice's advice
   (B) Upgrade his tools
   (C) Use paper tracking

17. Why does Ben think he avoided talking to the client?
   (A) To avoid disappointment
   (B) Because of time constraints
   (C) Due to a lack of trust

18. What type of project management tools does Alice suggest?
   (A) Simple and free ones
   (B) Advanced and real-time ones
   (C) Only digital ones

19. What does Alice believe about small wins in projects?
   (A) They are unimportant
   (B) They demotivate the team
   (C) They help with team morale

20. How does Ben feel about trying new project management tools?
   (A) Excited
   (B) Nervous
   (C) Indifferent

21. What does Alice think is beneficial about delegation?
    (A) It makes the project finish faster
    (B) It uses the team's strengths
    (C) It reduces overall workload

22. Why does Alice suggest a rotating schedule?
    (A) To promote responsibility
    (B) To reduce transparency
    (C) To eliminate all challenges

23. How does Ben describe his project management tool?
    (A) Advanced
    (B) Basic
    (C) Premium

24. How can setting milestones impact the team, according to Alice?
    (A) It slows them down
    (B) It keeps them motivated
    (C) It creates frustration

25. What advice does Alice give about client delays?
    (A) Avoid mentioning them
    (B) Discuss them transparently
    (C) Reduce the project scope

26. Why does Alice suggest notifying the client of delays?
   (A) It surprises them later
   (B) It prevents misunderstandings
   (C) It encourages complaints

27. What is Ben's plan for workload management?
   (A) Implement a rotating schedule
   (B) Do everything himself
   (C) Delay delegation

28. How does Alice describe the effect of transparent communication?
   (A) Builds trust
   (B) Causes delays
   (C) Creates confusion

29. What does Alice say about regular directory reviews?
   (A) Weekly
   (B) Monthly
   (C) Daily

30. What does Ben commit to by the end of the conversation?
   (A) Delegating all tasks
   (B) Avoiding client updates
   (C) Managing workload more effectively

〈Conversation Practice Answer Key〉

(1) (B)
(2) (B)
(3) (B)
(4) (B)
(5) (B)
(6) (B)
(7) (A)
(8) (B)
(9) (B)
(10) (B)
(11) (B)
(12) (A)
(13) (B)
(14) (B)
(15) (C)
(16) (B)
(17) (A)
(18) (B)
(19) (C)
(20) (A)
(21) (B)
(22) (A)
(23) (B)
(24) (B)
(25) (B)
(26) (B)
(27) (A)
(28) (A)
(29) (A)
(30) (C)

4 Paragraph Practice

Questions 1–4 refer to the following paragraph.

Jessica was assigned the task of resolving a client issue that had escalated recently. She first gathered all the necessary information to understand the 1. _______ of the problem. After analyzing the data, Jessica brainstormed possible solutions and prioritized them based on feasibility. Next, she 2. _______ with her team to get their feedback on the proposed solutions. Finally, she selected the most practical approach and prepared a detailed 3. _______ plan to ensure effective implementation. Jessica communicated the resolution steps clearly to the client, hoping to 4. _______ their confidence in her team.

1.

(A) depth (B) urgency
(C) nature (D) complexity

2.

(A) disagreed (B) collaborated
(C) dismissed (D) instructed

3.

(A) action (B) emergency
(C) backup (D) sales

4.

(A) discourage (B) restore
(C) damage (D) confirm

〈Paragraph Practice Answer Key〉

(1) (C)

(2) (B)

(3) (A)

(4) (B)

5 Idiom Practice

1. Bite the bullet – To face a difficult situation with courage.
   "She knew she had to bite the bullet and address the problem head-on."

2. Think outside the box – To approach a problem creatively.
   "We need to think outside the box to find a solution."

3. Put out fires – To deal with urgent problems.
   "Every day, she puts out fires with different client issues."

4. Weigh the pros and cons – To consider all aspects before deciding.
   "He weighed the pros and cons before making a choice."

5. The ball is in your court – It's your decision or responsibility to act.
   "Now the ball is in your court to resolve the issue."

6. On the back burner – To delay something until a later time.
   "They put less important tasks on the back burner."

7. Get down to brass tacks – Focus on the essential details.
   "Let's get down to brass tacks and solve this issue."

8. At the eleventh hour – At the last possible moment.
   "They resolved the issue at the eleventh hour."

9. A blessing in disguise – Something that seems bad but turns out beneficial.
   "Losing that client was a blessing in disguise."

10. Cut to the chase – Get to the point quickly.
    "Let's cut to the chase and discuss the decision-making process."

Chapter 5. Discussing Current Events

1 Dialogue Practice

John: Hi, Lisa. Did you catch the latest news about the economic summit?
Lisa: Yes, I did. It seems like there were some groundbreaking decisions made this time.

John: Absolutely. The trade agreements they reached could have a huge impact globally.
Lisa: I'm curious to see how it will affect our industry. What do you think?

John: Well, if tariffs are reduced, we might see a boost in international trade for sure.
Lisa: That would be great. But I'm also worried about the political implications.

John: True, it's a double-edged sword. Increased trade could lead to dependency on foreign markets.
Lisa: Exactly. And with the political climate being so unpredictable, it's a risky move.

John: Did you also hear about the new environmental regulations introduced?
Lisa: Yes, they're finally putting stricter limits on industrial emissions.

John: It's long overdue. Hopefully, it'll push companies to adopt cleaner technologies.
Lisa: I agree. But I wonder how realistic the implementation will be for smaller businesses.

John: Good point. Compliance might be challenging without government subsidies.

Lisa: Do you think there will be any backlash from the business community?

John: I expect so. Some industries might argue it increases operational costs significantly.

Lisa: That's true. Balancing economic growth with environmental sustainability is no easy task.

John: Right. It'll be interesting to see how they enforce these new standards.

Lisa: Enforcement has always been the weak point. Many companies find loopholes to avoid regulations.

John: That's unfortunate. Let's hope this time it's different.

Lisa: I think public pressure might help. People are more environmentally conscious now.

John: Definitely. Social media amplifies awareness, and companies can't ignore it.

Lisa: Speaking of social media, did you see the controversy surrounding the new privacy laws?

John: Yes, it's causing quite a stir. Many people feel their rights are being infringed upon.

Lisa: It's a tough balance between privacy and security, especially with rising cyber threats.

John: Exactly. The government argues that these laws are necessary for national security.

Lisa: But at what cost? Giving up privacy rights is a serious matter.

John: I think transparency is key here. People need to know exactly how their data is being used.

Lisa: Agreed. Without transparency, there will always be mistrust.

John: Do you think these laws will affect international relations?

Lisa: Possibly. Other countries might view it as a form of surveillance and react defensively.

John: That's a valid concern. It could lead to diplomatic tension if not handled carefully.

Lisa: Let's hope there's a balanced approach that respects both security and privacy.

John: It's a difficult situation. I guess only time will tell how it plays out.

Lisa: Indeed. Current events are changing so rapidly these days, it's hard to keep up.

John: That's true. Staying informed has become more essential than ever.

Lisa: Well, thanks for the discussion, John. It's always enlightening to hear your insights.

John: Anytime, Lisa. Let's stay updated and share more thoughts soon.

Lisa: Absolutely. Take care until next time.

2 Sentence Practice

(1) The trade agreements reached could have a global impact.

(2) Increased trade can lead to dependency on foreign markets.

(3) Stricter environmental regulations have been introduced.

(4) Compliance might be challenging for smaller businesses.

(5) Balancing economic growth with sustainability is difficult.

(6) Enforcement has often been the weak point of regulations.

(7) Social media amplifies awareness and influences companies.

(8) Privacy laws are causing public concern about rights.

(9) Transparency is key to reducing mistrust about data usage.

(10) International relations might be affected by new privacy laws.

3 Conversation Practice

1. What recent event are John and Lisa discussing at the start?
   (A) A sports championship
   (B) An economic summit
   (C) A new tech launch

2. What does John think reduced tariffs will lead to?
   (A) Less trade
   (B) Increased local production
   (C) A boost in international trade

3. Why is Lisa worried about increased trade?
   (A) It could lead to dependency on foreign markets
   (B) It might cause inflation
   (C) It could increase tariffs

4. What does Lisa mention about the political climate?
   (A) It's stable
   (B) It's unpredictable
   (C) It's irrelevant to trade

5. What new regulations did John hear about?
   (A) Environmental regulations
   (B) Import regulations
   (C) Tax regulations

6. Why does Lisa think smaller businesses might struggle?
   (A) They lack resources for compliance
   (B) They oppose all regulations
   (C) They are already following regulations

7. What is John's expectation from the business community?
   (A) Full support
   (B) Backlash due to costs
   (C) Indifference

8. Why do some companies avoid regulations, according to Lisa?
   (A) To save money
   (B) Due to lack of awareness
   (C) Because they are exempt

9. How does John feel about public pressure on companies?
   (A) It's useless
   (B) It's beneficial
   (C) It's overwhelming

10. What recent controversy on social media did Lisa mention?
   (A) New privacy laws
   (B) Business transparency
   (C) Environmental changes

11. How does John view the balance between privacy and security?
   (A) It's unnecessary
   (B) It's a difficult balance
   (C) It's easily achievable

12. What is the government's argument for the new privacy laws?
   (A) Economic benefit
   (B) National security
   (C) Increased employment

13. What does Lisa believe is essential for building trust?
   (A) Quick enforcement
   (B) Transparency
   (C) Financial incentives

14. What impact could privacy laws have on international relations, according to Lisa?
   (A) Increased cooperation
   (B) Diplomatic tension
   (C) Irrelevance

15. Why do other countries view privacy laws critically?
   (A) Due to high costs
   (B) Due to surveillance concerns
   (C) Due to limited impact

16. What does Lisa hope for in terms of privacy and security?
   (A) A balanced approach
   (B) Increased surveillance
   (C) No changes

17. How does Lisa describe the pace of current events?
   (A) Slow
   (B) Rapid
   (C) Static

18. What does John believe is essential today?
   (A) Staying informed
   (B) Avoiding the news
   (C) Ignoring global events

19. How does Lisa feel about discussing current events with John?
   (A) Bored
   (B) Enlightened
   (C) Indifferent

20. What does John plan to do to stay updated?
   (A) Watch only local news
   (B) Discuss more with Lisa
   (C) Avoid discussions

21. What does Lisa suggest about public opinion and companies?
   (A) Companies ignore it
   (B) It has a strong influence
   (C) It's irrelevant

22. What does John think about social media's role in awareness?
   (A) It reduces awareness
   (B) It amplifies awareness
   (C) It has no impact

23. How does John describe balancing privacy and security?
   (A) Easy
   (B) Challenging
   (C) Unnecessary

24. What does Lisa think might help in enforcing new laws?
   (A) Public pressure
   (B) Reduced regulations
   (C) Increased trade

25. How does Lisa feel about government transparency?
   (A) It's unimportant
   (B) It's crucial for trust
   (C) It should be reduced

26. What impact might the privacy laws have on businesses, according to John?
(A) Increased costs
(B) Decreased transparency
(C) Improved productivity

27. What does John think of companies avoiding regulations?
(A) It's justified
(B) It's unfortunate
(C) It's unavoidable

28. How does Lisa describe people's attitude towards the environment now?
(A) They're more conscious
(B) They're indifferent
(C) They're less aware

29. What does John say about companies and public opinion?
(A) They can't ignore it
(B) They disregard it
(C) They focus solely on profit

30. Why is Lisa interested in the economic summit's decisions?
(A) For economic growth only
(B) For political stability
(C) For their impact on her industry

〈Conversation Practice Answer Key〉

(1) (B)
(2) (C)
(3) (A)
(4) (B)
(5) (A)
(6) (A)
(7) (B)
(8) (A)
(9) (B)
(10) (A)
(11) (B)
(12) (B)
(13) (B)
(14) (B)
(15) (B)
(16) (A)
(17) (B)
(18) (A)
(19) (B)
(20) (B)
(21) (B)
(22) (B)
(23) (B)
(24) (A)
(25) (B)
(26) (A)
(27) (B)
(28) (A)
(29) (A)
(30) (C)

4 Paragraph Practice

Questions 1–4 refer to the following paragraph.

The recent climate conference brought together leaders from all over the world to discuss the pressing issue of climate change. The summit's focus was on reducing 1. _______ emissions, particularly from high-polluting industries. Many nations committed to increasing their use of 2. _______ energy to lower their carbon footprint. However, some countries expressed concern about the economic impact of such measures, particularly those reliant on fossil fuels. Overall, the summit ended with a plan to 3. _______ progress annually, ensuring accountability and 4. _______ across borders.

1.

(A) water (B) carbon
(C) natural (D) greenhouse

2.

(A) renewable (B) nuclear
(C) non-renewable (D) chemical

3.

(A) halt (B) ignore
(C) monitor (D) reduce

4.

(A) transparency (B) secrecy
(C) inconsistency (D) independence

〈Paragraph Practice Answer Key〉

(1) (B)

(2) (A)

(3) (C)

(4) (A)

5 Idiom Practice

1. Draw a line in the sand – Set a limit that must not be crossed.
   "Countries are drawing a line in the sand on environmental policies."

2. Walk a fine line – Balance between two difficult choices.
   "The government must walk a fine line between privacy and security."

3. Blow out of proportion – Exaggerate the importance of an issue.
   "The media blew the privacy laws debate out of proportion."

4. Get to the heart of – Understand the main issue deeply.
   "They got to the heart of the climate change debate."

5. Put one's foot down – Take a firm stand.
   "He put his foot down regarding the new privacy policies."

6. Raise red flags – Warn of potential issues or dangers.
   "The summit raised red flags about rising emissions."

7. In the limelight – Receive a lot of public attention.
   "The privacy laws are in the limelight this year."

8. Read the room – Understand the general mood or opinion.
   "Politicians need to read the room before implementing new laws."

9. Bend over backward – Make a great effort to accommodate.
   "Leaders are bending over backward to reach a consensus."

10. A tough pill to swallow – A difficult or unpleasant reality to accept.
    "The economic impact of climate policies is a tough pill to swallow."

Chapter 6. Science and Innovation

1 Dialogue Practice

Emma: Hi, Daniel. Did you hear about the new breakthrough in AI technology?

Daniel: Yes, I did. It's incredible how rapidly artificial intelligence is advancing these days.

Emma: Absolutely. They're now saying it can be used to diagnose medical conditions more accurately.

Daniel: That's a game-changer. Imagine the impact it could have on healthcare globally.

Emma: True. But there are still ethical questions around it, like privacy and data security.

Daniel: Definitely. With sensitive data involved, there's a lot to consider before widespread adoption.

Emma: And it's not just healthcare. They're also using AI in environmental conservation now.

Daniel: I read about that. AI drones are being used to monitor endangered species and illegal logging.

Emma: It's a fascinating application. Technology is becoming an essential tool in preservation efforts.

Daniel: But there's always the question of dependency. Are we relying too much on technology?

Emma: That's a valid concern. There needs to be a balance between innovation and practicality.

Daniel: I agree. Did you also read about the new energy-efficient batteries they're developing?

Emma: Yes! Those batteries could revolutionize how we store renewable energy.

Daniel: If they're able to scale production, it could lead to a significant reduction in fossil fuel reliance.

Emma: Right. And that would align perfectly with global sustainability goals.

Daniel: But as with all innovations, cost and accessibility are huge factors.

Emma: Exactly. Cutting-edge technology is often expensive at first, which limits its initial reach.

Daniel: Speaking of innovation, I heard they're experimenting with lab-grown meat again.

Emma: Yes, they're making progress. It might even become a common alternative in a few years.

Daniel: That could have a huge impact on the meat industry and on reducing environmental damage.

Emma: Indeed. If more people adopt it, it could change how we think about food production.

Daniel: And the health implications are interesting too. Lab-grown meat could be modified for better nutrition.

Emma: It's exciting to think about the future of food science. But do you think people will accept it?

Daniel: That's the big question. Public perception often dictates the success of new products.

Emma: I agree. People can be resistant to change, especially when it comes to food.

Daniel: But with the right education, I think acceptance is possible over time.

Emma: Education is key. And transparency from companies will be crucial as well.

Daniel: Exactly. Without transparency, people might mistrust the products.

Emma: By the way, have you been following the developments in space exploration?

Daniel: Yes, I have. The idea of commercial space travel is no longer science fiction.

Emma: It's amazing. Companies are already selling tickets for future space tourism.

Daniel: But there's the environmental impact to consider. Launches still rely heavily on fuel.

Emma: Good point. Sustainability will need to be addressed if space tourism is to become mainstream.

Daniel: And the cost is astronomical—pun intended. It's far from accessible to the average person.

Emma: True, but who knows? Maybe in a few decades, it'll be more affordable.

Daniel: Let's hope so. Science and innovation have a way of surprising us.

Emma: Indeed. The future holds so many possibilities, but also so many questions.

Daniel: That's what makes it exciting. We're on the cusp of things we never thought possible.

Emma: Yes, and it's amazing to witness these advancements in our lifetime.

2 Sentence Practice

(1) AI technology is advancing rapidly and transforming various industries.

(2) Ethical questions around privacy and data security remain challenging.

(3) AI is now used in environmental conservation, such as monitoring endangered species.

(4) Energy-efficient batteries could revolutionize renewable energy storage.

(5) Lab-grown meat could become a common alternative in the future.

(6) Public perception often determines the success of new products.

(7) Transparency from companies is crucial for public trust.

(8) Commercial space travel is now becoming a reality.

(9) Sustainability concerns arise with the impact of space tourism.

(10) Science and innovation continuously bring new possibilities and challenges.

3 Conversation Practice

1. What breakthrough did Emma mention at the beginning?
   (A) AI in medical diagnostics
   (B) Space travel
   (C) Lab-grown meat

2. What industry could be transformed by AI diagnosis?
   (A) Agriculture
   (B) Healthcare
   (C) Education

3. What ethical issue concerns Emma about AI?
   (A) Accessibility
   (B) Data security
   (C) Cost

4. How is AI used in environmental conservation?
   (A) By creating renewable energy
   (B) Monitoring endangered species
   (C) Making organic food

5. What innovation did Daniel mention regarding energy?
   (A) Solar panels
   (B) Energy-efficient batteries
   (C) Wind turbines

6. What could energy-efficient batteries reduce reliance on?
   (A) Solar energy
   (B) Fossil fuels
   (C) Nuclear energy

7. What does Emma say limits the reach of new technology?
   (A) High initial cost
   (B) Lack of interest
   (C) Inadequate infrastructure

8. What new food product is Emma interested in?
   (A) Organic vegetables
   (B) Lab-grown meat
   (C) Dairy alternatives

9. What industry could be impacted by lab-grown meat?
   (A) Meat industry
   (B) Technology sector
   (C) Automobile industry

10. What advantage does lab-grown meat offer in terms of nutrition?
   (A) It's free of fats
   (B) It can be modified for better nutrition
   (C) It's high in calories

11. How does Daniel think people might respond to lab-grown meat?
   (A) With acceptance
   (B) With excitement
   (C) With resistance

12. What could help in gaining public acceptance of lab-grown meat?
   (A) Heavy marketing
   (B) Educational campaigns
   (C) Reduced prices

13. Why does Emma believe transparency from companies is crucial?
   (A) To increase product availability
   (B) To build public trust
   (C) To reduce costs

14. What recent development in space did Emma mention?
   (A) Mars colonization
   (B) Commercial space travel
   (C) Space mining

15. What environmental concern does Daniel raise about space travel?
   (A) Pollution from launches
   (B) Noise pollution
   (C) Alien species disturbance

16. What aspect of space travel does Emma find problematic?
   (A) Availability
   (B) Accessibility due to high cost
   (C) Noise levels

17. How does Daniel feel about the future of space travel?
   (A) Indifferent
   (B) Hopeful
   (C) Worried

18. According to Daniel, what determines the success of new products?
   (A) Cost reduction
   (B) Public perception
   (C) Government support

19. Why does Emma think people might resist lab-grown meat?
   (A) It's expensive
   (B) It's unfamiliar as food
   (C) It's too nutritious

20. What is the biggest challenge in renewable energy storage?
   (A) Fuel availability
   (B) Battery efficiency
   (C) Lack of demand

21. How does Emma describe public response to lab-grown meat?
   (A) Enthusiastic
   (B) Skeptical
   (C) Neutral

22. What is Emma's primary concern regarding AI in healthcare?
   (A) Ethical implications
   (B) Treatment costs
   (C) Efficiency

23. What does Daniel say about commercial space travel's feasibility?
   (A) It's accessible
   (B) It's expensive
   (C) It's sustainable

24. What does Emma mention as the future of energy sources?
   (A) Nuclear power
   (B) Renewable energy
   (C) Natural gas

25. Why does Emma think energy-efficient batteries are important?
   (A) They are cheap
   (B) They help reduce fossil fuel use
   (C) They are easy to produce

26. What does Daniel think about innovation in food science?
   (A) It will be accepted without hesitation
   (B) It's interesting but will face resistance
   (C) It's unnecessary

27. Why is Emma excited about science and innovation?
   (A) They simplify life
   (B) They open new possibilities
   (C) They lower costs

28. How does Daniel think public opinion impacts product success?
   (A) It doesn't matter
   (B) It's essential
   (C) It's irrelevant

29. What's Emma's view on balancing innovation and practicality?
   (A) It's unimportant
   (B) It's challenging but necessary
   (C) It's unnecessary

30. What does Daniel think about the role of transparency?
   (A) It's irrelevant
   (B) It's essential for trust
   (C) It's easy to maintain

〈Conversation Practice Answer Key〉

(1) (A)
(2) (B)
(3) (B)
(4) (B)
(5) (B)
(6) (B)
(7) (A)
(8) (B)
(9) (A)
(10) (B)
(11) (C)
(12) (B)
(13) (B)
(14) (B)
(15) (A)
(16) (B)
(17) (B)
(18) (B)
(19) (B)
(20) (B)
(21) (B)
(22) (A)
(23) (B)
(24) (B)
(25) (B)
(26) (B)
(27) (B)
(28) (B)
(29) (B)
(30) (B)

4 Paragraph Practice

Questions 1–4 refer to the following paragraph.

At the recent innovation summit, experts discussed how advancements in 1. ______ are reshaping industries, from healthcare to environmental conservation. In particular, AI technology is now being used to 2. ______ endangered species populations, ensuring better data for protection efforts. Moreover, scientists are working on new energy-efficient 3. ______ that could change the future of renewable energy storage. As always, the issue of public acceptance and 4. ______ remains a critical factor in these technologies' success.

1.

(A) education (B) artificial intelligence
(C) construction (D) finance

2.

(A) increase (B) monitor
(C) replace (D) document

3.

(A) chemicals (B) solar panels
(C) batteries (D) food supplies

4.

(A) cost (B) transparency
(C) secrecy (D) demand

〈Paragraph Practice Answer Key〉

(1) (B)

(2) (B)

(3) (C)

(4) (B)

5 Idiom Practice

1. Ahead of the curve – Being more advanced or innovative than others.
"Our company always tries to stay ahead of the curve in technology."

2. Push the envelope – To go beyond normal limits.
"This new design really pushes the envelope in terms of energy efficiency."

3. Jump on the bandwagon – To follow a trend once it becomes popular.
"Many companies are jumping on the AI bandwagon."

4. Break new ground – To innovate or pioneer in a particular field.
"The researchers broke new ground in renewable energy storage."

5. In the pipeline – Something in development or pending.
"There are several new products in the pipeline for this year."

6. Level the playing field – Make something fair or accessible for everyone.
"AI in education could help level the playing field for students."

7. Hit the ground running – Start a task energetically and effectively.
"With this technology, we can hit the ground running on our project."

8. Back to the drawing board – Rethink or redesign something from scratch.
"The prototype failed, so it's back to the drawing board."

9. Keep one's finger on the pulse – Stay updated on trends and changes.
"You need to keep your finger on the pulse of industry advancements."

10. Think outside the box – To be creative or unconventional.
"Solving this issue requires thinking outside the box."

Chapter 7. History and Culture

1 Dialogue Practice

Emma: Hi, Daniel. Are you planning to go to the history exhibit at the museum this weekend?

Daniel: Yes, I am. I've heard it's an impressive collection, with artifacts from ancient civilizations.

Emma: That sounds fascinating. I've always been interested in ancient history.

Daniel: Me too. There's something about understanding past cultures that enriches our view of the present.

Emma: Absolutely. I think it helps us understand our own culture better.

Daniel: Did you know they have a special section on the Egyptian civilization?

Emma: Really? The Egyptian culture is one of my favorites. Their achievements were remarkable.

Daniel: I agree. The ancient Egyptians had a profound impact on science, architecture, and art.

Emma: Do they also have exhibits from other ancient civilizations?

Daniel: Yes, they do. There's a section dedicated to the Greek and Roman empires.

Emma: The Greeks and Romans contributed so much to philosophy and government.

Daniel: And don't forget their contributions to literature and theater.

Emma: Of course. I love reading classical literature. Do they have anything on the Middle Ages?

Daniel: Yes, they have a section on medieval Europe. There's a focus on feudal society and the role of religion.

Emma: That must be interesting. The Middle Ages was a transformative period in history.

Daniel: Indeed. The changes that occurred then laid the foundation for the modern world.

Emma: It's amazing to think about how much has evolved since then.

Daniel: Speaking of evolution, they also have an exhibit on the Renaissance period.

Emma: Ah, the Renaissance! A rebirth of arts, culture, and science.

Daniel: Exactly. That period produced some of the greatest minds in history.

Emma: I'd love to see any works by da Vinci or Michelangelo if they have any replicas.

Daniel: I'm sure they do. The Renaissance was truly a golden age for art.

Emma: Do they have any exhibits related to Asian cultures?

Daniel: Yes, there's an entire wing dedicated to Asian history and culture, including ancient China, Japan, and India.

Emma: Ancient Asian civilizations had such rich philosophies and advanced technologies.

Daniel: They did. The Chinese, for instance, invented paper, gunpowder, and the compass.

Emma: And India contributed greatly in mathematics and philosophy.
Daniel: It's inspiring to see how interconnected world history is.

Emma: That's true. Every culture has left a mark on the world in some way.
Daniel: I believe understanding history fosters respect for other cultures.

Emma: I agree. Learning about history encourages tolerance and appreciation.
Daniel: Do you think schools should focus more on cultural history?

Emma: Definitely. History lessons often focus too much on dates rather than cultural impacts.
Daniel: Well, this exhibit seems to cover both in a balanced way.

Emma: It sounds like a perfect weekend plan. I can't wait to see it.
Daniel: Me too. Shall we go together?

Emma: Yes, I'd love that. Let's make sure to take our time at each exhibit.
Daniel: Agreed. It's not every day we get to see such a comprehensive display.

Emma: By the way, have you visited the museum's ancient art section?
Daniel: No, I haven't. What's it like?

Emma: It's incredible. They have artifacts from prehistory, including early tools and sculptures.
Daniel: That sounds amazing. I wonder how humans created art without modern tools.

Emma: It's a testament to human ingenuity and creativity.
Daniel: Indeed. Humans have always found ways to express themselves through art.

Emma: It's one of the things that connects us to our ancestors.

Daniel: Art truly is a universal language.

Emma: I'm glad we're both passionate about history and culture.

Daniel: Me too. It's great to have a friend who shares the same interests.

2 Sentence Practice

(1) Understanding past cultures enriches our view of the present.

(2) Ancient Egyptian achievements were remarkable in science and art.

(3) The Middle Ages laid the foundation for the modern world.

(4) The Renaissance was a golden age for art and science.

(5) Every culture has left a mark on the world in some way.

(6) Learning about history encourages tolerance and appreciation.

(7) Ancient China contributed inventions like paper and the compass.

(8) History fosters respect for different cultures.

(9) Art is a universal language that connects us to our ancestors.

(10) Studying history helps us understand our own culture better.

3 Conversation Practice

1. What type of exhibit is Daniel planning to attend?
   (A) Art exhibit
   (B) History exhibit
   (C) Science exhibit

2. Which ancient civilization does Emma mention as her favorite?
   (A) Egyptian
   (B) Greek
   (C) Roman

3. What did the ancient Egyptians contribute to?
   (A) Literature
   (B) Philosophy
   (C) Science and architecture

4. What civilizations have a dedicated section in the exhibit?
   (A) Only Egyptian
   (B) Greek and Roman
   (C) Chinese and Indian

5. What period does Daniel mention as a focus on feudal society?
   (A) The Renaissance
   (B) The Middle Ages
   (C) The Modern Era

6. What does Emma call the Renaissance?
   (A) A dark age
   (B) A rebirth of arts and culture
   (C) A peaceful era

7. What is Emma hoping to see replicas of?
   (A) Paintings by Picasso
   (B) Works by da Vinci or Michelangelo
   (C) Artifacts from prehistoric times

8. Which Asian countries are included in the exhibit?
   (A) Only China
   (B) Japan, China, and India
   (C) Korea and Thailand

9. What did the Chinese invent according to Daniel?
   (A) Medicine
   (B) Gunpowder and the compass
   (C) Philosophy

10. What subject does Emma feel is underrepresented in schools?
   (A) Cultural history
   (B) World geography
   (C) Modern literature

11. How does Daniel describe the museum's display?
   (A) Minimalistic
   (B) Comprehensive
   (C) Unbalanced

12. What section of the museum does Emma recommend?
   (A) Medieval artifacts
   (B) Ancient art
   (C) Modern art

13. What aspect of art does Emma believe connects us to ancestors?
   (A) Language
   (B) Architecture
   (C) Expression through art

14. How does Daniel view art?
   (A) As a universal language
   (B) As a modern creation
   (C) As a science

15. What does Emma say about learning history?
   (A) It's boring
   (B) It encourages tolerance
   (C) It's irrelevant

16. Which period does Daniel think had significant scientific achievements?
   (A) The Renaissance
   (B) The Modern Era
   (C) The Middle Ages

17. Why is Emma excited about the museum visit?
   (A) She loves architecture
   (B) She loves history
   (C) She loves science

18. Who invented paper according to the dialogue?
   (A) Indians
   (B) Egyptians
   (C) Chinese

19. What does Daniel consider art to be?
   (A) A cultural divider
   (B) A universal language
   (C) A modern phenomenon

20. How does Emma view history in terms of cultural respect?
   (A) As irrelevant
   (B) As fostering respect
   (C) As outdated

21. What ancient tool is mentioned in the conversation?
   (A) Compass
   (B) Paintbrush
   (C) Microscope

22. Where does Emma suggest they take their time?
   (A) At each exhibit
   (B) Only at the art exhibit
   (C) Only at the Renaissance section

23. Which civilization contributed to philosophy according to Emma?
   (A) Egyptians
   (B) Romans
   (C) Greeks

24. What role does Daniel attribute to education in public acceptance?
   (A) Minimal
   (B) Significant
   (C) Unnecessary

25. What innovation in art does Emma admire?
   (A) Use of modern tools
   (B) Early human creativity without modern tools
   (C) Only Renaissance art

26. What did Emma say about the Middle Ages?
   (A) It was a peaceful time
   (B) It was a transformative period
   (C) It was irrelevant

27. Why is the Renaissance called a "rebirth"?
   (A) It was peaceful
   (B) It revived arts, culture, and science
   (C) It promoted feudalism

28. What is Emma's viewpoint on cultural history in schools?
   (A) It's irrelevant
   (B) It needs more focus
   (C) It's overly emphasized

29. How does Daniel view ancient history?
   (A) As irrelevant
   (B) As insightful
   (C) As fictional

30. What does Daniel enjoy most about history?
   (A) Memorizing dates
   (B) Understanding culture
   (C) Analyzing architecture

〈Conversation Practice Answer Key〉

(1) (B)
(2) (A)
(3) (C)
(4) (B)
(5) (B)
(6) (B)
(7) (B)
(8) (B)
(9) (B)
(10) (A)
(11) (B)
(12) (B)
(13) (C)
(14) (A)
(15) (B)
(16) (A)
(17) (B)
(18) (C)
(19) (B)
(20) (B)
(21) (A)
(22) (A)
(23) (C)
(24) (B)
(25) (B)
(26) (B)
(27) (B)
(28) (B)
(29) (B)
(30) (B)

4 Paragraph Practice

Questions 1–4 refer to the following paragraph.

In recent years, museums have increased their focus on showcasing the culture and history of lesser-known civilizations. At a local exhibit, visitors can explore artifacts from 1. ______ and learn about their daily lives and beliefs. These displays also highlight the influence of 2. ______ on these ancient cultures, from religion to art. A notable exhibit emphasizes how trade routes connected these civilizations, allowing for the exchange of 3. ______ across continents. Overall, the goal is to foster 4. ______ and awareness of these unique contributions to human history.

1.

(A) modern Europe
(B) ancient Persia
(C) medieval France
(D) futuristic societies

2.

(A) science
(B) agriculture
(C) technology
(D) religion

3.

(A) goods
(B) myths
(C) music
(D) games

4.

(A) indifference
(B) cultural appreciation
(C) criticism
(D) isolation

〈Paragraph Practice Answer Key〉

(1) (B)

(2) (D)

(3) (A)

(4) (B)

5 Idiom Practice

1. Know the ropes – To be familiar with the ins and outs of something.
   "After studying ancient history, he really knows the ropes of historical analysis."

2. Put yourself in someone's shoes – To imagine experiencing someone else's life.
   "When learning about ancient cultures, try to put yourself in their shoes."

3. Break the mold – To do something in a new way, unlike anything before.
   "Ancient artists broke the mold with their unique styles and techniques."

4. Old as the hills – Very old or ancient.
   "Some traditions are as old as the hills but still relevant today."

5. In the same boat – Sharing a similar experience or situation.
   "Many ancient civilizations were in the same boat with trade challenges."

6. Set in stone – Permanent or fixed.
   "Certain cultural practices were set in stone for centuries."

7. Bring to the table – To contribute to a situation or discussion.
   "Each civilization brings unique achievements to the table."

8. See eye to eye – To agree on something.
   "Historians don't always see eye to eye on interpretations of history."

9. A blast from the past – Something that brings back memories of the past.

"Seeing ancient artifacts feels like a blast from the past."

10. Throw in the towel – To give up or stop trying.

"Despite many invasions, some civilizations refused to throw in the towel."

Chapter 8. Social Issues and Volunteering

1 Dialogue Practice

Emma: Hi, Jacob. I heard you're involved in some volunteer work. Could you tell me more about it?

Jacob: Sure, Emma. I volunteer at a local food bank every Saturday. It's quite fulfilling.

Emma: That sounds wonderful. What inspired you to start volunteering?

Jacob: I realized how fortunate I am, and I wanted to give back to the community.

Emma: That's a noble reason. Do you work with a lot of other volunteers?

Jacob: Yes, there's a dedicated team. Many are students, while others are working professionals.

Emma: It must be a great team effort. What kinds of tasks do you usually handle?

Jacob: We sort food donations, pack bags, and sometimes help with distribution.

Emma: Is it hard to balance volunteering with your other commitments?

Jacob: It can be challenging, but I find the time because it's something I care about deeply.

Emma: How does the food bank operate? Do they rely solely on donations?

Jacob: Mostly, yes. They also receive support from local businesses and grants.

Emma: That's good to hear. Do you think the community appreciates the work you all do?

Jacob: Absolutely. People are incredibly grateful, which makes it all worth it.

Emma: I can imagine. I've been thinking of getting involved in volunteer work myself.

Jacob: That's fantastic! There are so many organizations in need of volunteers.

Emma: Do you have any suggestions on where to start?

Jacob: Well, think about causes you care about. Then, find local organizations focused on those areas.

Emma: I'm passionate about environmental issues. Maybe I could help with a cleanup initiative.

Jacob: That's a great idea. Many cities have programs focused on environmental conservation.

Emma: Do you think it's easy to find time for volunteering?

Jacob: I believe it's a matter of prioritizing. If you value it, you'll make time for it.

Emma: That's true. How did you get started with the food bank?

Jacob: I saw a flyer about their need for volunteers, and I decided to give it a try.

Emma: Have you had any memorable experiences while volunteering?

Jacob: Plenty! Meeting people from different backgrounds has been very eye-opening.

Emma: That's amazing. It sounds like volunteering has changed your perspective.
Jacob: It certainly has. I've become more aware of social issues and how they affect people.

Emma: Do you think more people should get involved in community service?
Jacob: Definitely. Even a small amount of time can make a significant difference.

Emma: I agree. What other types of volunteer work interest you?
Jacob: I'd like to work with youth organizations, helping kids with their studies.

Emma: That's a noble goal. Education is such an important area to support.
Jacob: Absolutely. Education empowers people to overcome many social barriers.

Emma: Have you thought about organizing your own volunteer group?
Jacob: Yes, that's something I've considered, especially to address specific community needs.

Emma: That would be impressive. How would you go about starting a group?
Jacob: I'd begin by reaching out to like-minded people and organizing regular meetings.

Emma: That sounds doable. Have you faced any challenges in volunteering?
Jacob: Sometimes, resources are limited, and it's hard to meet everyone's needs.

Emma: That must be tough. How do you handle those situations?
Jacob: We do the best we can with what we have and try to find additional support.

Emma: Do you think you'll continue volunteering long-term?
Jacob: Absolutely. It's become an essential part of my life.

Emma: That's inspiring. I hope to follow in your footsteps and make a difference.
Jacob: I'm sure you will, Emma. There's always room for more people who want to help.

Emma: Thanks for the encouragement, Jacob. I'll start looking for opportunities.
Jacob: Anytime, Emma. Volunteering can be incredibly rewarding; I'm glad you're interested.

2 Sentence Practice

(1) I volunteer at a local food bank every Saturday.

(2) I wanted to give back to the community and help those in need.

(3) Many volunteers are students or working professionals.

(4) We sort food donations and help with distribution at the food bank.

(5) Volunteering has changed my perspective on social issues.

(6) People are incredibly grateful for the support we provide.

(7) I believe volunteering is about prioritizing and making time for it.

(8) Environmental issues are a popular cause for volunteers.

(9) Education empowers people to overcome social barriers.

(10) There's always room for more people who want to make a difference.

3 Conversation Practice

1. (A) At a hospital
   (B) At a food bank
   (C) At a school

2. How often does Jacob volunteer?
   (A) Every Saturday
   (B) Every weekday
   (C) Every month

3. Who does Jacob say are among the volunteers?
   (A) Only students
   (B) Mostly retired people
   (C) Students and working professionals

4. What tasks does Jacob handle at the food bank?
   (A) Cooking meals
   (B) Sorting donations
   (C) Teaching classes

5. What inspires Emma to consider volunteering?
   (A) Her friends volunteer
   (B) She's inspired by Jacob's experience
   (C) She has free time

6. What cause is Emma passionate about?
   (A) Health issues
   (B) Environmental issues
   (C) Animal welfare

7. What does Jacob suggest Emma do to start volunteering?
   (A) Contact the food bank
   (B) Find a cause she cares about
   (C) Join his team

8. How did Jacob learn about the food bank?
   (A) Through a friend
   (B) Through a flyer
   (C) On social media

9. What kind of volunteer work would Jacob like to try in the future?
   (A) Environmental cleanup
   (B) Teaching youth
   (C) Animal rescue

10. How does Jacob feel about balancing volunteering with other commitments?
   (A) It's difficult and tiring
   (B) It's manageable with prioritization
   (C) It's too challenging

11. What impact has volunteering had on Jacob?
   (A) He's become more understanding of social issues
   (B) He feels more stressed
   (C) He has less time for hobbies

12. Why does Jacob think more people should volunteer?
   (A) It helps improve society
   (B) It's a way to make money
   (C) It's an easy job

13. What type of organization would Emma consider joining?
   (A) An environmental cleanup group
   (B) A sports team
   (C) A youth organization

14. How does Jacob suggest starting a volunteer group?
   (A) By finding funding
   (B) By reaching out to like-minded people
   (C) By contacting the government

15. What is one challenge Jacob has faced in volunteering?
   (A) Limited resources
   (B) Lack of interest from the community
   (C) Lack of personal time

16. How does Jacob describe the people they serve at the food bank?
   (A) Wealthy
   (B) Grateful
   (C) Unfriendly

17. What other area of volunteer work does Jacob consider important?
   (A) Sports
   (B) Education
   (C) Marketing

18. What advice does Jacob give about finding time for volunteering?
   (A) Sacrifice sleep
   (B) Make it a priority
   (C) Quit other activities

19. What does Emma think volunteering will do for her?
   (A) Provide relaxation
   (B) Allow her to meet new people
   (C) Make her more socially aware

20. What motivates Jacob to continue volunteering?
   (A) It's easy
   (B) He loves helping others
   (C) He has nothing else to do

21. How does Jacob feel about volunteering long-term?
   (A) He wants to stop soon
   (B) He's committed to it
   (C) He's unsure

22. Where would Emma like to volunteer?
   (A) At a museum
   (B) With an environmental group
   (C) At a hospital

23. What type of volunteer work would Jacob consider organizing?
   (A) Educational programs for youth
   (B) Political events
   (C) Real estate workshops

24. What does Jacob say about the impact of small volunteer efforts?
   (A) They don't matter
   (B) They make a difference
   (C) They're a waste of time

25. How does Emma feel after talking to Jacob?
   (A) Inspired to volunteer
   (B) Indifferent
   (C) Reluctant

26. What other social issue does Jacob mention?
    (A) Political reform
    (B) Community education
    (C) Healthcare access

27. What does Jacob do when resources are limited?
    (A) Stops volunteering
    (B) Looks for additional support
    (C) Ignores the issue

28. Who inspired Jacob to start volunteering?
    (A) His family
    (B) Himself
    (C) A friend

29. What skill does Jacob hope to improve by working with youth?
    (A) Leadership
    (B) Teaching
    (C) Fundraising

30. How does Jacob feel about the gratitude people express at the food bank?
    (A) It makes him feel fulfilled
    (B) It's overwhelming
    (C) It's unnecessary

〈Conversation Practice Answer Key〉

(1) (B)
(2) (A)
(3) (C)
(4) (B)
(5) (B)
(6) (B)
(7) (B)
(8) (B)
(9) (B)
(10) (B)
(11) (A)
(12) (A)
(13) (A)
(14) (B)
(15) (A)
(16) (B)
(17) (B)
(18) (B)
(19) (C)
(20) (B)
(21) (B)
(22) (B)
(23) (A)
(24) (B)
(25) (A)
(26) (B)
(27) (B)
(28) (B)
(29) (B)
(30) (A)

4 Paragraph Practice

Questions 1–4 refer to the following paragraph.

Community centers have been struggling to find enough volunteers to help with 1. _______. Many people are unaware of the range of services these centers offer, from youth programs to 2. _______ workshops for adults. The centers have tried various strategies, including social media campaigns and community events, to attract more volunteers. Still, the shortage persists, especially during holiday seasons when more individuals need support. To address this issue, some centers are considering offering 3. _______ training sessions for new volunteers to increase interest and prepare them for their roles. The goal is to build a reliable volunteer base that can effectively assist with community services, fostering a sense of 4. _______ among members.

1.

(A) administration　(B) outreach
(C) counseling　(D) legal advice

2.

(A) cooking　(B) language
(C) technical　(D) social

3.

(A) extensive　(B) costly
(C) brief　(D) unnecessary

4.

(A) division　(B) collaboration
(C) isolation　(D) indifference

〈Paragraph Practice Answer Key〉

(1) (B)

(2) (C)

(3) (A)

(4) (B)

5 Idiom Practice

1. Go the extra mile – To make an extra effort beyond what is expected.
   "Volunteers are known to go the extra mile to help those in need."

2. Lend a hand – To offer help or assistance.
   "Whenever there's a community event, people are eager to lend a hand."

3. Give back – To contribute to one's community or society.
   "He wanted to give back by helping at the local shelter."

4. Do one's bit – To do one's part in a collective effort.
   "Everyone can do their bit to make the world a better place."

5. In the same boat – Facing a similar situation as others.
   "All volunteers were in the same boat during the busy holiday season."

6. Step up to the plate – To take responsibility for a task.
   "When they needed more volunteers, she stepped up to the plate."

7. Take it upon oneself – To decide to do something without being asked.
   "He took it upon himself to organize a community cleanup."

8. Make a difference – To have a positive impact on a situation.
   "Every small action can make a difference in someone's life."

9. Pull together – To work cooperatively to achieve a goal.
   "Everyone pulled together to make the charity event a success."

10. Rally the troops – To gather people together for a common cause.
   "The community leader rallied the troops for the weekend volunteer event."

Chapter 9. Time Management

1 Dialogue Practice

Lisa: Hi, Tom. I noticed you always manage to get your work done on time. What's your secret?

Tom: Hi, Lisa. Well, I prioritize tasks based on deadlines and importance.

Lisa: That's smart. I sometimes struggle to keep track of everything.

Tom: Have you tried using a planner or a digital calendar?

Lisa: I use a digital calendar, but I often forget to check it.

Tom: Setting reminders can help. I set multiple alerts for crucial tasks.

Lisa: Good idea. Do you set aside specific times for certain activities?

Tom: Yes, I block out time in my schedule for focused work, meetings, and breaks.

Lisa: I should try that. How do you handle unexpected tasks?

Tom: I leave some flexibility in my schedule for those. It's important to stay adaptable.

Lisa: Makes sense. Do you set goals for each day?

Tom: Absolutely. I have a to-do list with daily, weekly, and monthly goals.

Lisa: That's impressive! I tend to get overwhelmed by long to-do lists.

Tom: Try breaking down large tasks into smaller steps. It feels more manageable that way.

Lisa: I'll give it a shot. How do you avoid distractions?

Tom: I set specific times for checking emails and messages instead of looking at them constantly.

Lisa: That's a great strategy. I often get sidetracked by notifications.

Tom: You can also silence non-essential notifications during work hours.

Lisa: I hadn't thought of that. Do you take breaks often?

Tom: Yes, regular breaks help me recharge. I follow the Pomodoro Technique sometimes.

Lisa: I've heard of that. It's 25 minutes of work followed by a 5-minute break, right?

Tom: Exactly. It's effective for maintaining focus over long periods.

Lisa: Do you set long-term goals too?

Tom: Yes, having a clear vision helps me stay motivated and aligned with my objectives.

Lisa: How do you track your progress?

Tom: I review my goals weekly to see what I've accomplished and what needs more attention.

Lisa: That's helpful. I feel like I often lose track of time when working.

Tom: Using a timer can help with that. It keeps you aware of how long you've been on a task.

Lisa: Good point. Do you ever feel overwhelmed by deadlines?

Tom: Occasionally, but I remind myself to take things one step at a time.

Lisa: It sounds like you have a well-organized approach. Do you plan everything?
Tom: Not everything. I like to leave some room for spontaneity and creativity.

Lisa: That's a good balance. How do you handle days when things don't go as planned?
Tom: I adapt and try to focus on what I can control instead of stressing over setbacks.

Lisa: Great advice. Do you use any apps for time management?
Tom: Yes, I use a few. My favorites are for task tracking and reminders.

Lisa: Thanks for sharing. I'll look into those. Do you set personal goals along with work goals?
Tom: Yes, it's important to balance both. Personal goals keep me grounded.

Lisa: That's a good perspective. I feel like I need a better work-life balance.
Tom: Boundaries are essential. I set a time to finish work and stick to it as much as possible.

Lisa: I'll try that. How do you handle procrastination?
Tom: I start with the easiest task to build momentum or set a timer to get started.

Lisa: Do you reward yourself for completing tasks?
Tom: Yes, rewards motivate me. Even small rewards can make a difference.

Lisa: That's encouraging. Thank you, Tom. I'll start implementing these ideas.
Tom: Anytime, Lisa. Time management takes practice, but it's worth the effort.

Lisa: I agree. I'm excited to improve my productivity.

2 Sentence Practice

(1) I prioritize tasks based on deadlines and importance.

(2) Setting reminders can help keep you on track.

(3) I block out time in my schedule for focused work and breaks.

(4) Breaking down large tasks into smaller steps can make them more manageable.

(5) Regular breaks help me recharge and maintain focus.

(6) I follow the Pomodoro Technique to balance work and rest.

(7) Having a clear vision for long-term goals keeps me motivated.

(8) I review my goals weekly to track my progress.

(9) Setting boundaries is essential for work-life balance.

(10) Rewards, even small ones, motivate me to stay productive.

3 Conversation Practice

1. What tool does Tom recommend for tracking tasks?
   (A) A digital calendar
   (B) A physical notebook
   (C) A timer

2. What strategy does Tom use to avoid distractions?
   (A) Taking longer breaks
   (B) Setting specific times for emails
   (C) Working without breaks

3. How often does Tom review his goals?
   (A) Daily
   (B) Weekly
   (C) Monthly

4. What technique does Tom follow to manage his time?
   (A) Time Blocking
   (B) The Pomodoro Technique
   (C) Just-in-time strategy

5. What is one way Tom stays adaptable in his schedule?
   (A) Leaving flexibility for unexpected tasks
   (B) Ignoring last-minute changes
   (C) Following a strict plan

6. How does Tom track the time he spends on tasks?
   (A) Using a timer
   (B) Setting an alarm
   (C) Writing it down

7. What is Tom's view on long-term goals?
   (A) He doesn't set them
   (B) They're important for motivation
   (C) They're unnecessary

8. How does Tom handle overwhelming tasks?
   (A) He ignores them
   (B) He breaks them into smaller steps
   (C) He delegates them

9. What does Tom use as motivation to complete tasks?
   (A) Rewards
   (B) Reminders
   (C) Deadlines

10. How does Lisa feel about Tom's approach to time management?
   (A) Inspired
   (B) Unimpressed
   (C) Confused

11. What does Lisa use to track her tasks?
   (A) A digital calendar
   (B) A paper planner
   (C) Sticky notes

12. Why does Lisa sometimes struggle with her schedule?
   (A) She's too busy
   (B) She forgets to check her calendar
   (C) She doesn't set reminders

13. What does Tom suggest Lisa silence during work?
   (A) Her phone
   (B) Non-essential notifications
   (C) Emails

14. What method does Tom suggest for tackling procrastination?
   (A) Starting with an easy task
   (B) Taking a break first
   (C) Ignoring deadlines

15. How does Tom feel about days that don't go as planned?
   (A) He stresses out
   (B) He tries to adapt
   (C) He ignores them

16. What does Lisa want to improve through time management?
   (A) Her work-life balance
   (B) Her email response time
   (C) Her exercise routine

17. What does Tom do to ensure he doesn't feel overwhelmed?
   (A) He completes everything in one go
   (B) He focuses on one step at a time
   (C) He takes long breaks

18. What is Lisa's response to Tom's reward system?
   (A) She's encouraged
   (B) She disagrees
   (C) She's skeptical

19. How does Tom handle notifications?
   (A) He ignores them
   (B) He checks them immediately
   (C) He silences non-essential ones

20. What advice does Tom give for building momentum?
   (A) Start with the hardest task
   (B) Start with the easiest task
   (C) Don't start at all

21. How does Tom prevent burnout?
   (A) By working continuously
   (B) By taking regular breaks
   (C) By setting longer hours

22. What approach does Tom use for large tasks?
   (A) Delegating them
   (B) Ignoring them
   (C) Breaking them down

23. How does Lisa feel about her current approach to tasks?
   (A) Overwhelmed
   (B) Confident
   (C) Relaxed

24. What app feature does Tom mention using?
   (A) Task tracking
   (B) Social media updates
   (C) Virtual meetings

25. Why does Lisa want to improve her productivity?
   (A) She has too much free time
   (B) She wants to be more organized
   (C) She wants a new job

26. What does Tom suggest Lisa do with her work boundaries?
    (A) Set a finishing time
    (B) Work continuously
    (C) Work late every day

27. How does Tom describe setting reminders?
    (A) As distracting
    (B) As helpful
    (C) As unnecessary

28. What does Lisa plan to implement first?
    (A) Setting boundaries
    (B) Task delegation
    (C) Working without breaks

29. How does Tom view spontaneity in his schedule?
    (A) He ignores it
    (B) He incorporates it for creativity
    (C) He thinks it's disruptive

30. What is Tom's outlook on time management?
    (A) It takes constant practice
    (B) It's impossible to master
    (C) It's unimportant

〈Conversation Practice Answer Key〉

(1) (A)
(2) (B)
(3) (B)
(4) (B)
(5) (A)
(6) (A)
(7) (B)
(8) (B)
(9) (A)
(10) (A)
(11) (A)
(12) (B)
(13) (B)
(14) (A)
(15) (B)
(16) (A)
(17) (B)
(18) (A)
(19) (C)
(20) (B)
(21) (B)
(22) (C)
(23) (A)
(24) (A)
(25) (B)
(26) (A)
(27) (B)
(28) (A)
(29) (B)
(30) (A)

4 Paragraph Practice

Questions 1-4 refer to the following paragraph.

Managing time effectively is a crucial skill in both personal and professional settings. One popular method is the Pomodoro Technique, which involves working for short periods followed by brief 1. ______. This technique helps in maintaining focus and preventing burnout. Another approach is time blocking, where individuals dedicate specific blocks of time to 2. ______ tasks without interruptions. People who follow this method often report increased productivity. In addition to these, setting realistic goals and prioritizing 3. ______ tasks can make a significant difference in managing one's time. Ultimately, the goal is to achieve a balance that allows for both productivity and 4. ______.

1.

(A) sessions (B) breaks
(C) delays (D) meetings

2.

(A) various (B) minor
(C) specific (D) flexible

3.

(A) short-term (B) secondary
(C) priority (D) long-term

4.

(A) stress (B) leisure
(C) advancement (D) urgency

〈Paragraph Practice Answer Key〉

(1) (B)

(2) (C)

(3) (C)

(4) (B)

5 Idiom Practice

1. Beat the clock – To finish something before a deadline.
   "We managed to beat the clock and submit the report early."

2. On the back burner – To delay or postpone something.
   "We put that project on the back burner for now."

3. The eleventh hour – At the last possible moment.
   "He finished his part at the eleventh hour."

4. Under the gun – Under pressure to complete something.
   "She's really under the gun to finish her work."

5. Tick all the boxes – To meet all requirements.
   "This plan ticks all the boxes for time management."

6. Burn the midnight oil – To work late into the night.
   "She had to burn the midnight oil to get the job done."

7. Ahead of the curve – To be more advanced than the others.
   "With her time management skills, she's ahead of the curve."

8. Keep your eye on the ball – To stay focused on a goal.
   "He kept his eye on the ball and finished his tasks."

9. Time flies – Time passes quickly.
   "Time flies when you're focused and productive."

10. Race against time – A situation where something must be done very quickly.
    "It was a race against time to meet the deadline."

Chapter 10. Business English Basics

1 Dialogue Practice

Megan: Hi, Alex. I wanted to discuss the recent project deadlines. Have you noticed any issues?

Alex: Hi, Megan. Yes, I noticed a few bottlenecks, especially in the marketing phase.

Megan: I thought so. Do you think we should adjust the timeline?

Alex: I believe so. A slight extension might improve the quality of our output.

Megan: Agreed. Have you informed the team about this possibility?

Alex: Not yet. I wanted to discuss it with you first before making any announcements.

Megan: That's considerate. When do you think would be a good time to tell them?

Alex: I think at the weekly meeting. It would give everyone a chance to share their input.

Megan: Good idea. Do you think everyone is on board with the project goals?

Alex: Most of them, yes. But I think a few team members are struggling to keep up.

Megan: Should we provide them with additional resources or support?

Alex: That might be helpful. It could make a big difference in their productivity.

Megan: I'll talk to HR about arranging some training sessions. Would you be willing to lead one?

Alex: Sure, I'd be happy to. I think I can help simplify some of the complex areas.

Megan: Great! How is your own workload? Are you managing okay?

Alex: It's been intense, but manageable. I just need to prioritize effectively.

Megan: If you need any assistance, please let me know.

Alex: Thank you, Megan. I appreciate your support.

Megan: By the way, are there any budget constraints on this project?

Alex: Yes, the finance team has requested that we keep costs under strict control.

Megan: I expected that. Let's try to cut any unnecessary expenses.

Alex: Agreed. We could reduce the number of external consultations.

Megan: Good thinking. What about the software licenses we discussed?

Alex: I'm working on negotiating lower prices with our vendors.

Megan: Excellent! Do you think we'll still come in under budget?

Alex: It's going to be tight, but I think it's achievable with careful planning.

Megan: Let's keep monitoring it closely. Also, do you have any updates on the project's timeline?

Alex: We're on track for now, but it's best to remain cautious.

Megan: Absolutely. Let's aim to complete this project on time and within budget.

Alex: That's the goal. It will make a great impression on our clients.

Megan: Yes, and it will show the team's capabilities. Are there any potential risks you foresee?

Alex: A few, mainly related to the supply chain. Delays could impact our timeline.

Megan: Let's keep a close eye on that and have a backup plan in place.

Alex: Agreed. I'll work with logistics to ensure everything is on schedule.

Megan: Perfect. I feel confident about this project. Let's keep up the good work.

Alex: Yes, let's stay focused. I'll follow up with you on the updates next week.

Megan: Sounds good. Thank you, Alex. I appreciate your dedication.

Alex: Thank you, Megan. Together, we'll make this project a success.

2 Sentence Practice

(1) A slight extension might improve the quality of our output.

(2) I wanted to discuss the recent project deadlines with you.

(3) Providing additional resources could increase productivity.

(4) It's important to keep costs under strict control.

(5) Let's aim to complete this project on time and within budget.

(6) A backup plan can mitigate potential risks in the supply chain.

(7) Negotiating lower prices with vendors could help reduce expenses.

(8) Keeping a close eye on the timeline is essential to meet deadlines.

(9) We need to ensure that all team members understand the project goals.

(10) Effective prioritization helps manage a heavy workload.

3 Conversation Practice

1. What aspect of the project is causing a bottleneck?
   (A) Marketing phase
   (B) Product design
   (C) Software development

2. Why does Megan suggest adjusting the timeline?
   (A) To reduce costs
   (B) To improve output quality
   (C) To add more team members

3. When does Alex propose to inform the team about the timeline adjustment?
   (A) Today
   (B) After the meeting
   (C) At the weekly meeting

4. What support does Megan plan to arrange for the team?
   (A) Financial aid
   (B) Additional training
   (C) Marketing materials

5. Who might lead a training session for the team?
   (A) HR Manager
   (B) Alex
   (C) Megan

6. What has the finance team requested regarding the project?
   (A) Increase spending
   (B) Extend the deadline
   (C) Control costs strictly

7. What does Megan suggest to help stay under budget?
   (A) Cut unnecessary expenses
   (B) Increase sales
   (C) Hire more staff

8. How does Alex plan to reduce software costs?
   (A) By negotiating with vendors
   (B) By removing features
   (C) By hiring new developers

9. How does Megan want the team to handle project risks?
   (A) Ignore them
   (B) Address them without a backup plan
   (C) Monitor and create a backup plan

10. What might delay the project timeline, according to Alex?
   (A) Budget issues
   (B) Supply chain delays
   (C) Marketing strategies

11. What motivates the team to complete the project on time?
   (A) To impress clients
   (B) To receive a bonus
   (C) To avoid extra work

12. What could make a big difference in team productivity?
   (A) A tighter deadline
   (B) Additional resources
   (C) Reduced working hours

13. How does Alex plan to keep costs down?
   (A) By reducing the team size
   (B) By reducing consultations
   (C) By lowering the quality

14. When will Alex follow up with Megan on updates?
   (A) Next week
   (B) Next month
   (C) Tomorrow

15. Who requested lower prices for software licenses?
   (A) Finance team
   (B) Alex
   (C) Megan

16. What's Megan's view on the project budget?
    (A) It's unlimited
    (B) It should be carefully controlled
    (C) It doesn't matter

17. How does Megan feel about the project's progress?
    (A) Uncertain
    (B) Confident
    (C) Uninvolved

18. What's Alex's main responsibility regarding logistics?
    (A) Ignore any issues
    (B) Ensure everything is on schedule
    (C) Delegate it to Megan

19. How often does Megan review the project budget?
    (A) Daily
    (B) Weekly
    (C) Monthly

20. What is one major risk Alex foresees?
    (A) Budget overrun
    (B) Supply chain delays
    (C) Poor teamwork

21. What impression does Megan hope the project will leave?
   (A) It shows the team's capabilities
   (B) It shows the limitations of the team
   (C) It won't matter to the clients

22. How does Alex handle his workload?
   (A) By prioritizing effectively
   (B) By working overtime
   (C) By ignoring tasks

23. Who decides on the additional training sessions?
   (A) HR
   (B) Megan
   (C) Alex

24. How does Alex feel about his workload?
   (A) Overwhelmed
   (B) Manageable
   (C) Ignored

25. What does Alex think about completing the project under budget?
   (A) It's not achievable
   (B) It's possible with careful planning
   (C) It's easy to do

26. What will happen if unnecessary expenses are reduced?
   (A) The project will slow down
   (B) Budget will be more controlled
   (C) The quality will decrease

27. Who is responsible for communicating with vendors?
   (A) Megan
   (B) Finance team
   (C) Alex

28. What does Alex say about the current timeline?
   (A) It's delayed
   (B) It's on track but requires caution
   (C) It needs an extension

29. What motivates Megan's leadership style?
   (A) Avoiding stress
   (B) Ensuring team involvement
   (C) Maximizing budget

30. Who initially noticed the project bottleneck?
   (A) HR department
   (B) Alex
   (C) Finance team

〈Conversation Practice Answer Key〉

(1) (A)
(2) (B)
(3) (C)
(4) (B)
(5) (B)
(6) (C)
(7) (A)
(8) (A)
(9) (C)
(10) (B)
(11) (A)
(12) (B)
(13) (B)
(14) (A)
(15) (B)
(16) (B)
(17) (B)
(18) (B)
(19) (B)
(20) (B)
(21) (A)
(22) (A)
(23) (A)
(24) (B)
(25) (B)
(26) (B)
(27) (C)
(28) (B)
(29) (B)
(30) (B)

4 Paragraph Practice

Questions 1-4 refer to the following paragraph.

Karen is managing a complex project with multiple stakeholders, including clients, vendors, and team members. She started by 1. _______ the project's objectives with her team to ensure everyone understood their responsibilities. Karen held regular meetings to 2. _______ any issues that might arise and encourage team members to share feedback. By doing so, she hoped to 3. _______ productivity and minimize risks. However, she noticed that managing 4. _______ among the stakeholders was challenging, as each had different expectations.

1.
(A) finalizing (B) communicating
(C) defining (D) avoiding

2.
(A) ignore (B) avoid
(C) address (D) amplify

3.
(A) enhance (B) restrict
(C) lower (D) delay

4.
(A) collaboration (B) feedback
(C) interaction (D) meetings

〈Paragraph Practice Answer Key〉

(1) (B)

(2) (C)

(3) (A)

(4) (A)

5 Idiom Practice

1. Put all your eggs in one basket – To risk everything on a single opportunity.
   "Relying on one client for income is putting all your eggs in one basket."

2. Play hardball – To be tough and ruthless in negotiations.
   "He had to play hardball to get the best deal."

3. By the book – To do things according to the rules.
   "They handled the process by the book to avoid any issues."

4. Get the ball rolling – To start something.
   "Let's get the ball rolling on this project."

5. Go the extra mile – To make an extra effort.
   "She's always willing to go the extra mile for her clients."

6. Think outside the box – To think creatively.
   "We need to think outside the box for this project."

7. Back to square one – To start over.
   "After the failure, we are back to square one."

8. Cut corners – To save time or money by doing something quickly.
   "Cutting corners may lead to poor results."

9. Learn the ropes – To understand how to do a job or activity.
   "It took him a while to learn the ropes in his new position."

10. Take the bull by the horns – To confront a problem directly.
    "She decided to take the bull by the horns and address the issue."

Chapter 11. Making Appointments and Schedules

1 Dialogue Practice

Sarah: Hi, Mark. I wanted to confirm our meeting schedule for next week.
Mark: Sure, Sarah. What time were you thinking?

Sarah: I was hoping we could meet on Tuesday morning. Does that work for you?
Mark: Tuesday morning is a bit packed for me. How about Wednesday afternoon?

Sarah: Wednesday could work. Shall we say around 2 p.m.?
Mark: That's perfect. I'll add it to my calendar.

Sarah: Great. I'll make sure I'm prepared. Is there anything specific you'd like to discuss?
Mark: Yes, I'd like to go over the project timeline and any possible adjustments.

Sarah: Sounds good. I'll bring the latest updates with me.
Mark: Excellent. By the way, how's your schedule looking for the rest of the week?

Sarah: It's fairly busy, but I should be able to make time for other meetings if needed.
Mark: I appreciate that. We might need to schedule another follow-up meeting.

Sarah: No problem. I'll keep my calendar open for that.
Mark: Thanks, Sarah. Are you planning to review the client's feedback beforehand?

Sarah: Absolutely. I'll go over it in detail before our meeting.
Mark: That's a good idea. I think it'll help us address any concerns efficiently.

Sarah: Agreed. Are you also going to bring the financial projections?
Mark: Yes, I'll have them ready. I know they're a crucial part of the discussion.

Sarah: Excellent. By the way, should we invite anyone else to join?
Mark: Let's keep it between us for now, unless we need additional input.

Sarah: Understood. And are we sticking to our usual meeting room?
Mark: Yes, it's already booked for us.

Sarah: Perfect. I'll be there a few minutes early to set up.
Mark: Great. If anything changes, I'll give you a heads-up.

Sarah: Thanks, Mark. I'll do the same.
Mark: One last thing—should we plan for an hour, or will we need more time?

Sarah: Let's schedule an hour and adjust if necessary.
Mark: Sounds good. I'll block out that time.

Sarah: Thanks for coordinating this, Mark. It helps keep things organized.
Mark: My pleasure, Sarah. Looking forward to a productive meeting.

Sarah: Same here. See you Wednesday at 2.
Mark: See you then!

2 Sentence Practice

(1) I wanted to confirm our meeting schedule for next week.

(2) Let's plan for an hour and adjust if necessary.

(3) I'll bring the latest updates with me to the meeting.

(4) Are you also going to bring the financial projections?

(5) I'll review the client's feedback before our discussion.

(6) Is there anything specific you'd like to discuss in the meeting?

(7) I'll be there a few minutes early to set up.

(8) We should address any client concerns efficiently.

(9) Should we invite anyone else to join us for this meeting?

(10) My schedule is fairly busy, but I can make time if needed.

3 Conversation Practice

1. When does Sarah propose to meet?
   (A) Monday morning
   (B) Tuesday morning
   (C) Wednesday afternoon

2. What time does Mark suggest instead?
   (A) Tuesday afternoon
   (B) Wednesday morning
   (C) Wednesday afternoon

3. What does Sarah plan to bring to the meeting?
   (A) Financial projections
   (B) Project updates
   (C) Client reports

4. What aspect of the project does Mark want to discuss?
   (A) Budget
   (B) Timeline
   (C) Marketing

5. Why will Sarah review the client's feedback beforehand?
   (A) To make adjustments
   (B) To address concerns efficiently
   (C) To impress the client

6. How long does Sarah suggest the meeting should last?
   (A) 30 minutes
   (B) 1 hour
   (C) 2 hours

7. Who is responsible for bringing the financial projections?
   (A) Sarah
   (B) Mark
   (C) The finance team

8. Where will the meeting take place?
   (A) In the usual meeting room
   (B) At a new location
   (C) Online

9. What is Mark's role in setting up the meeting?
   (A) He is arranging the meeting room.
   (B) He is coordinating the schedule.
   (C) He is reviewing the project budget.

10. Who suggests inviting others to the meeting?
   (A) Mark
   (B) Sarah
   (C) The HR department

11. How does Sarah respond to the suggestion of inviting others?
  (A) She agrees immediately.
  (B) She suggests postponing it.
  (C) She agrees to keep it between them.

12. What day and time is the meeting finally scheduled?
  (A) Tuesday at 2 p.m.
  (B) Wednesday at 2 p.m.
  (C) Thursday at 10 a.m.

13. Why does Mark ask about Sarah's schedule for the rest of the week?
  (A) To arrange a follow-up meeting
  (B) To reschedule their current meeting
  (C) To plan a project deadline

14. How does Sarah show she's prepared for the meeting?
  (A) By asking specific questions
  (B) By confirming her attendance
  (C) By offering to review client feedback

15. What does Mark agree to give if there are any changes?
  (A) A written report
  (B) A heads-up
  (C) A project extension

16. Who will arrive early to set up for the meeting?
   (A) Mark
   (B) Sarah
   (C) An assistant

17. What is Sarah's attitude towards her busy schedule?
   (A) She's frustrated.
   (B) She's flexible.
   (C) She's indifferent.

18. Who is coordinating the meeting schedule?
   (A) HR
   (B) Mark
   (C) Sarah

19. What will they discuss during the meeting?
   (A) Financial projections and client feedback
   (B) Marketing strategies only
   (C) Sales reports only

20. How does Mark feel about the project timeline?
   (A) Confident
   (B) Uncertain
   (C) Uninterested

21. hat does Sarah plan to do before the meeting?
   (A) Arrive late
   (B) Review feedback
   (C) Prepare a presentation

22. Why might they schedule a follow-up meeting?
   (A) To finish discussing the project
   (B) To meet with more team members
   (C) To discuss budget issues

23. Who will keep an open schedule for follow-up meetings?
   (A) Sarah
   (B) Mark
   (C) Both

24. How does Sarah feel about Mark's coordination efforts?
   (A) She's grateful.
   (B) She's indifferent.
   (C) She's critical.

25. Why does Mark ask about Sarah's workload?
   (A) To offer assistance
   (B) To reschedule their meeting
   (C) To check her commitment

26. Who brings up the importance of efficiency?
  (A) Sarah
  (B) Mark
  (C) The finance team

27. What will Mark do if anything changes in the schedule?
  (A) Inform Sarah
  (B) Notify HR
  (C) Reschedule the meeting entirely

28. What does Sarah appreciate about Mark?
  (A) His dedication
  (B) His financial expertise
  (C) His sense of humor

29. When will they discuss potential project adjustments?
  (A) During the meeting
  (B) At the end of the month
  (C) Next quarter

30. Who confirms the final time for the meeting?
  (A) Mark
  (B) Sarah
  (C) Both

〈Conversation Practice Answer Key〉

(1) (B)
(2) (C)
(3) (B)
(4) (B)
(5) (B)
(6) (B)
(7) (B)
(8) (A)
(9) (B)
(10) (B)
(11) (C)
(12) (B)
(13) (A)
(14) (C)
(15) (B)
(16) (B)
(17) (B)
(18) (B)
(19) (A)
(20) (A)
(21) (B)
(22) (A)
(23) (C)
(24) (A)
(25) (A)
(26) (A)
(27) (A)
(28) (A)
(29) (A)
(30) (C)

4 Paragraph Practice

Questions 1–4 refer to the following paragraph.

David is working on creating a meeting schedule for the upcoming project. He begins by 1. _______ the availability of each team member to ensure everyone can attend. Once he has this information, he plans to send out a preliminary agenda that outlines the 2. _______ for the meeting. David knows that timing is crucial, as delays could impact the project's overall timeline. Finally, he will confirm the 3. _______ of the meeting with the team and provide them with any necessary preparation materials. David believes that an organized schedule is essential for maximizing 4. _______ during the meeting.

1.

(A) arranging　　(B) confirming

(C) scheduling　　(D) checking

2.

(A) goals　　(B) tasks

(C) structure　　(D) objective

3.

(A) time　　(B) location

(C) date　　(D) frequency

4.

(A) productivity　　(B) cooperation

(C) discussion　　(D) communication

〈Paragraph Practice Answer Key〉

(1) (D)

(2) (C)

(3) (B)

(4) (A)

5 Idiom Practice

1. Pencil in – To make a tentative appointment.
   "I'll pencil in the meeting for Thursday and confirm later."

2. Block out time – To reserve a specific period in your schedule.
   "He blocked out time to work on the presentation."

3. Play it by ear – To decide something based on the situation.
   "We'll play it by ear if we can't finalize the schedule."

4. Catch up – To review or go over recent developments.
   "Let's catch up on where we stand with the project."

5. Ahead of the curve – To be ahead in planning or progress.
   "She's always ahead of the curve with her scheduling."

6. On the same page – To be in agreement on a plan.
   "Let's ensure we're all on the same page before we begin."

7. In the loop – To stay informed about developments.
   "Please keep me in the loop about any changes."

8. Square away – To organize or complete tasks.
   "Let's square away the details before the meeting."

9. Touch base – To briefly connect and share updates.
   "I'll touch base with you about the schedule tomorrow."

10. Get the ball rolling – To initiate something.
    "Let's get the ball rolling on the meeting agenda."

Olivia: That's exciting! Do you feel nervous before an exhibition?

James: A little, but I've learned to embrace it as part of the process.

Olivia: How do you decide on the themes for each series?

James: I try to reflect on current events, personal experiences, or emotions I want to express.

Olivia: That's a very thoughtful approach. What do you find most challenging in your creative process?

James: Sometimes, it's the initial idea. Getting started can be daunting.

Olivia: I imagine it must be. Do you ever feel like you have artist's block?

James: Occasionally, but I try to work through it by experimenting with new techniques.

Olivia: That sounds like a great way to push through. What's your favorite medium to work with?

James: I enjoy both acrylic and watercolor, but each medium brings something different.

Olivia: I noticed that in your work. You seem to have mastered both.

James: Thank you. I still have a lot to learn, though.

Olivia: Do you have any plans to try new styles or mediums in the future?

James: Absolutely. I believe exploring new avenues is essential for growth.

Olivia: I completely agree. How do you handle feedback on your work?

James: I try to take constructive criticism positively; it helps me improve.

Chapter 12. Art and Creativity

1 Dialogue Practice

Olivia: Hi, James. I was hoping to discuss your recent artwork series. It's truly captivating.

James: Thank you, Olivia. I put a lot of thought into this series. What did you think of it?

Olivia: I loved the use of colors and textures. Each piece feels so alive and dynamic.

James: I'm glad you felt that way. I wanted to convey a sense of movement and emotion.

Olivia: Did you draw inspiration from any particular artist or style?

James: Not exactly. I wanted this series to be an expression of my own vision.

Olivia: It's very unique. How long did it take you to complete the entire series?

James: About three months, but I was working on multiple pieces at once.

Olivia: That must have required a lot of dedication. How do you stay motivated?

James: Art has always been my passion, so I don't need much motivation to keep going.

Olivia: That's wonderful. Are you planning to showcase these pieces in a gallery?

James: Yes, I have a few exhibitions lined up next month.

Olivia: That's exciting! Do you feel nervous before an exhibition?

James: A little, but I've learned to embrace it as part of the process.

Olivia: How do you decide on the themes for each series?

James: I try to reflect on current events, personal experiences, or emotions I want to express.

Olivia: That's a very thoughtful approach. What do you find most challenging in your creative process?

James: Sometimes, it's the initial idea. Getting started can be daunting.

Olivia: I imagine it must be. Do you ever feel like you have artist's block?

James: Occasionally, but I try to work through it by experimenting with new techniques.

Olivia: That sounds like a great way to push through. What's your favorite medium to work with?

James: I enjoy both acrylic and watercolor, but each medium brings something different.

Olivia: I noticed that in your work. You seem to have mastered both.

James: Thank you. I still have a lot to learn, though.

Olivia: Do you have any plans to try new styles or mediums in the future?

James: Absolutely. I believe exploring new avenues is essential for growth.

Olivia: I completely agree. How do you handle feedback on your work?

James: I try to take constructive criticism positively; it helps me improve.

Olivia: That's a good perspective. Do you have a favorite piece in this series?
James: It's hard to choose, but I'd say the one with the blue and orange contrast.

Olivia: That one is stunning. I can see why it stands out to you.
James: Thanks. What about you? Do you have a favorite?

Olivia: I loved the one with the forest scene. It feels so serene.
James: I wanted it to evoke a sense of calm and introspection.

Olivia: It definitely achieves that. What message do you hope your audience takes away?
James: I hope it inspires them to look at the world differently.

Olivia: That's a beautiful message. Do you see yourself as an artist primarily, or do you have other creative pursuits?
James: Art is my primary focus, but I also dabble in photography and sculpture.

Olivia: That's impressive! How do you manage to balance multiple creative projects?
James: I try to allocate time for each, but it's definitely a juggling act.

Olivia: It sounds like it. Do you find inspiration in other artists' work?
James: Absolutely. I love exploring art galleries and learning from others.

Olivia: That's wonderful. I feel like creativity often feeds off of other creativity.
James: I couldn't agree more. It's a continuous cycle of inspiration.

Olivia: Well, I'm excited to see where your journey takes you next.
James: Thank you, Olivia. I appreciate your interest and support.

2 Sentence Practice

(1) Each piece feels so alive and dynamic, capturing a sense of movement.

(2) I loved the use of colors and textures in your latest series.

(3) Art has always been my passion, so I find motivation in the process itself.

(4) I wanted this series to express my own vision without any particular influence.

(5) Sometimes, getting started with a new piece can be the most daunting part.

(6) I enjoy both acrylic and watercolor, as each medium brings something unique.

(7) Constructive criticism helps me grow and improve as an artist.

(8) The forest scene piece evokes a sense of calm and introspection.

(9) I hope my work inspires people to look at the world differently.

(10) Creativity is a continuous cycle of inspiration from various sources.

3 Conversation Practice

1. What did Olivia think of James's recent artwork series?
   (A) She found it dull.
   (B) She found it captivating.
   (C) She disliked it.

2. Where does James draw his inspiration from?
   (A) Other artists
   (B) His own vision
   (C) Famous art styles

3. How long did it take James to complete the series?
   (A) One month
   (B) Two months
   (C) Three months

4. What emotion does James aim to convey through his work?
   (A) Humor
   (B) Movement and emotion
   (C) Sadness

5. Where does James plan to showcase his work?
   (A) At a gallery
   (B) Online only
   (C) He has no plans to showcase it

6. How does James handle pre-exhibition nerves?
   (A) He ignores them.
   (B) He embraces them as part of the process.
   (C) He cancels the exhibition.

7. What theme does James use for his series?
   (A) Current events and personal experiences
   (B) Abstract themes
   (C) Simple landscapes

8. What is James's biggest challenge in his creative process?
   (A) Finishing pieces
   (B) The initial idea
   (C) Marketing his work

9. How does James work through artist's block?
   (A) He quits for a while.
   (B) He tries new techniques.
   (C) He waits until it passes.

10. Which medium does James prefer?
   (A) Acrylic
   (B) Charcoal
   (C) Both acrylic and watercolor

11. How does Olivia feel about James's use of color?
    (A) She loves it.
    (B) She dislikes it.
    (C) She finds it boring.

12. Does James enjoy trying new styles?
    (A) Yes, he finds it essential for growth.
    (B) No, he sticks to one style.
    (C) He hasn't tried anything new.

13. How does James view feedback on his work?
    (A) He ignores it.
    (B) He takes it constructively.
    (C) He resents it.

14. What is James's favorite piece in this series?
    (A) The forest scene
    (B) The blue and orange contrast
    (C) He has no favorite

15. How does Olivia describe the forest scene?
    (A) As serene
    (B) As chaotic
    (C) As colorful

16. What message does James hope his audience takes away?
   (A) To appreciate art
   (B) To view the world differently
   (C) To focus on colors

17. What other creative pursuits does James have?
   (A) Photography and sculpture
   (B) Acting
   (C) Only painting

18. How does James balance multiple creative projects?
   (A) By working only on one at a time
   (B) By managing his time carefully
   (C) By ignoring other projects

19. Does James find inspiration in other artists?
   (A) No
   (B) Sometimes
   (C) Yes

20. How does James feel about the continuous cycle of inspiration?
   (A) He finds it exhausting.
   (B) He believes it's essential.
   (C) He doesn't think it's necessary.

21. What does Olivia love about the series?
    (A) The dynamic colors and textures
    (B) The calmness
    (C) The abstract nature

22. What kind of art does Olivia describe as "serene"?
    (A) The forest scene
    (B) The abstract pieces
    (C) The blue and orange contrast

23. Where does James get his ideas for each series?
    (A) From others' opinions
    (B) From reflection on emotions
    (C) From his favorite artists

24. What is James's approach to learning and improving?
    (A) Ignoring criticism
    (B) Listening to feedback
    (C) Following trends

25. What does James hope his audience will do after seeing his art?
    (A) Feel happy
    (B) Think differently
    (C) Learn to paint

26. How does Olivia support James's career?
    (A) By buying his artwork
    (B) By giving constructive feedback
    (C) By encouraging him

27. Why does James think trying new mediums is essential?
    (A) For more sales
    (B) For artistic growth
    (C) For faster production

28. What theme does James explore in his forest scene?
    (A) Chaos
    (B) Reflection and calmness
    (C) Abstract ideas

29. Who has exhibitions lined up next month?
    (A) Olivia
    (B) James
    (C) Both of them

30. What does Olivia find most intriguing about James's work?
    (A) His attention to detail
    (B) His creative style
    (C) His marketing skills

〈Conversation Practice Answer Key〉

(1) (B)
(2) (B)
(3) (C)
(4) (B)
(5) (A)
(6) (B)
(7) (A)
(8) (B)
(9) (B)
(10) (C)
(11) (A)
(12) (A)
(13) (B)
(14) (B)
(15) (A)
(16) (B)
(17) (A)
(18) (B)
(19) (C)
(20) (B)
(21) (A)
(22) (A)
(23) (B)
(24) (B)
(25) (B)
(26) (C)
(27) (B)
(28) (B)
(29) (B)
(30) (B)

4 Paragraph Practice

Questions 1-4 refer to the following paragraph.

Emma recently completed her first solo art exhibition, showcasing a collection of vibrant landscapes. She aimed to capture the beauty of nature, with each piece highlighting a different season. Throughout the 1. _______ process, Emma refined her techniques, often experimenting with color and texture. The exhibition was well-received, with many viewers 2. _______ the depth of emotion in each painting. Emma felt a sense of 3. _______ as she observed people connecting with her work. She hopes her art will 4. _______ others to see the natural world in a new way.

1.

(A) learning (B) refining

(C) creative (D) interactive

2.

(A) admiring (B) questioning

(C) ignoring (D) analyzing

3.

(A) satisfaction (B) insecurity

(C) doubt (D) frustration

4.

(A) allow (B) encourage

(C) force (D) prevent

〈Paragraph Practice Answer Key〉

(1) (C)

(2) (A)

(3) (A)

(4) (B)

5 Idiom Practice

1. Brush up on – To improve or refine a skill.
   "I need to brush up on my painting techniques."

2. Think outside the box – To approach a problem creatively.
   "Artists are always encouraged to think outside the box."

3. Break the mold – To do something differently.
   "She broke the mold with her unique art style."

4. In the spotlight – To receive a lot of attention.
   "Her work was in the spotlight during the exhibition."

5. A blank canvas – Something that has endless possibilities.
   "Every new project is like a blank canvas."

6. Draw a line – To set a boundary.
   "He draws a line between his work and personal life."

7. Color outside the lines – To be unconventional.
   "Her art really colors outside the lines."

8. Out of the blue – Unexpectedly.
   "Out of the blue, she received an invitation to exhibit her work."

9. A work of art – Something exceptionally good.
   "His speech was a work of art in its own right."

10. Frame of mind – A particular mood or attitude.
    "She needs to be in the right frame of mind to create."

Chapter 13. Future Trends and Goal Setting

1 Dialogue Practice

Rachel: Hi, David. I heard you're working on some new goals for your team.
David: Hi, Rachel. Yes, we're looking at ways to stay ahead of industry trends.

Rachel: That sounds ambitious. Do you start by analyzing past performance?
David: Exactly. It helps us understand what worked and what didn't.

Rachel: Are you focusing on any particular trends this time?
David: We're looking closely at sustainability and digital transformation.

Rachel: Those are hot topics. Do you think they'll impact your team directly?
David: Definitely. We want to be proactive rather than reactive.

Rachel: What's the first step in your strategy?
David: Setting clear, measurable goals for each quarter.

Rachel: How do you ensure the goals are achievable yet challenging?
David: We try to align them with our resources and market opportunities.

Rachel: How often do you review the goals?
David: Quarterly, but we stay flexible in case we need to adjust.

Rachel: That's a smart approach. Do you involve your team in the planning?
David: Absolutely. Their input is invaluable.

Rachel: How do you keep them motivated throughout the process?
David: By setting milestones and recognizing achievements along the way.

Rachel: Do you think the market trends will change quickly?
David: They always do, which is why adaptability is key.

Rachel: What tools are you using to track progress?
David: Mainly project management software and data analytics.

Rachel: Do you foresee any challenges in implementing your strategy?
David: Managing resources and time will be challenging.

Rachel: How do you prioritize the trends to focus on?
David: We look at long-term impact and alignment with our values.

Rachel: Do you think these trends will shape the industry?
David: Absolutely. They're transforming how businesses operate.

Rachel: What about future goals? Are they set in stone?
David: Not at all. We revisit and revise them as needed.

Rachel: How do you decide when to revise your goals?
David: If market conditions change or we hit a major milestone.

Rachel: Are there any specific achievements you're aiming for?
David: We'd like to be industry leaders in sustainability.

Rachel: That's an impressive goal. What drives that ambition?
David: We want to make a positive impact while growing our business.

Rachel: How do you ensure the goals align with the company vision?
David: We evaluate each goal against our mission and values.

Rachel: Have you ever faced resistance to new trends?
David: Occasionally, but we address concerns through open communication.

Rachel: What's your approach to dealing with resistance?
David: Listening to feedback and demonstrating the benefits.

Rachel: Do you think goal-setting will evolve with technology?
David: Definitely. Data will make goal-setting even more precise.

Rachel: Do you track personal goals the same way as professional ones?
David: I try to, but personal goals are often more flexible.

Rachel: How do you balance immediate needs with long-term goals?
David: By setting priorities and timeframes for each objective.

Rachel: Do you find it hard to predict future trends?
David: It's challenging, but research and data make it manageable.

Rachel: How do you respond when goals aren't met?
David: We analyze what went wrong and make adjustments.

Rachel: What advice would you give to someone setting their first goals?
David: Start small, focus on consistency, and be open to change.

2 Sentence Practice

(1) Setting clear and measurable goals for each quarter is crucial for progress.

(2) We need to stay proactive to keep up with industry changes.

(3) Analyzing past performance helps in identifying what worked well.

(4) Sustainability and digital transformation are major trends to watch.

(5) Adaptability is essential in a fast-changing market.

(6) Regular reviews help keep goals relevant and achievable.

(7) Involving the team in planning increases their commitment.

(8) Recognizing achievements along the way keeps motivation high.

(9) Market conditions often require quick adjustments to goals.

(10) Being an industry leader requires both ambition and resilience.

3 Conversation Practice

1. What is David currently working on?
   (A) Team expansion
   (B) New goals for his team
   (C) Hiring new employees

2. How does David start his planning process?
   (A) By setting deadlines
   (B) By analyzing past performance
   (C) By hiring consultants

3. What trends is David focusing on?
   (A) Financial stability
   (B) Employee engagement
   (C) Sustainability and digital transformation

4. What is David's goal-setting strategy?
   (A) Set goals annually
   (B) Set clear and measurable goals quarterly
   (C) Set vague goals for flexibility

5. How often does David review the team's goals?
   (A) Annually
   (B) Monthly
   (C) Quarterly

6. How does David ensure the goals are realistic?
   (A) By aligning them with resources and market opportunities
   (B) By setting low standards
   (C) By ignoring the market

7. What motivates David's team during goal achievement?
   (A) Financial bonuses only
   (B) Setting milestones and recognizing achievements
   (C) Working overtime

8. How does David prioritize trends?
   (A) By their impact on revenue only
   (B) Based on long-term impact and alignment with values
   (C) Randomly

9. What tools does David use to track progress?
   (A) Manual tracking
   (B) Project management software and data analytics
   (C) Phone calls

10. How does David handle changing goals?
   (A) He ignores changes
   (B) He adjusts them as needed
   (C) He waits until the end of the year

11. Why does David involve his team in planning?
  (A) For compliance purposes
  (B) He values their input
  (C) He has no choice

12. What kind of goals does David's team have?
  (A) Unclear and flexible
  (B) Strict and unchanging
  (C) Clear and aligned with company values

13. How does David handle resistance to new trends?
  (A) By forcing changes
  (B) By listening and explaining the benefits
  (C) By ignoring it

14. Why does David believe adaptability is important?
  (A) The market is static
  (B) Trends change quickly
  (C) His team demands it

15. What does David consider the most challenging part of goal setting?
  (A) Managing resources and time
  (B) Finding new clients
  (C) Conducting interviews

16. How does David respond to unmet goals?
   (A) He ignores them
   (B) He analyzes the situation and adjusts
   (C) He blames his team

17. How does David's team know if they are on track?
   (A) Through regular communication and reviews
   (B) By guessing
   (C) By reviewing annually

18. What specific achievement is David aiming for?
   (A) To complete projects faster
   (B) To be a sustainability leader
   (C) To expand internationally

19. How does David view the role of technology in goal setting?
   (A) As an inconvenience
   (B) As essential for precision
   (C) As irrelevant

20. How does David balance immediate and long-term goals?
   (A) By focusing on only one type
   (B) By setting priorities and timeframes
   (C) By ignoring immediate goals

21. What does David think will impact future goal-setting?
   (A) Customer preferences
   (B) Technological advancements
   (C) Employee satisfaction

22. How does David track his personal goals?
   (A) He doesn't track them
   (B) Similar to his professional goals
   (C) With minimal tracking

23. Why does David set milestones for his team?
   (A) To track progress and celebrate achievements
   (B) To measure their productivity
   (C) To determine their bonuses

24. What does David consider when setting new goals?
   (A) Personal opinions only
   (B) The market and company resources
   (C) Only past trends

25. What advice does David give about setting goals?
   (A) Start big and be ambitious
   (B) Start small and be consistent
   (C) Ignore consistency

26. What does David believe about future trends in the industry?
   (A) They are stable
   (B) They change rapidly
   (C) They don't matter

27. How does David respond to industry changes?
   (A) By adjusting goals
   (B) By ignoring them
   (C) By consulting his team only

28. What's David's approach to employee involvement in goal-setting?
   (A) He doesn't involve them
   (B) He values their input
   (C) He uses their input only for minor goals

29. Why does David use analytics in his planning?
   (A) To predict the future accurately
   (B) To help with precise goal-setting
   (C) To avoid unnecessary meetings

30. What type of goals does David believe are essential for success?
   (A) Short-term only
   (B) Long-term only
   (C) A mix of both immediate and future goals

〈Conversation Practice Answer Key〉

(1) (B)
(2) (B)
(3) (C)
(4) (B)
(5) (C)
(6) (A)
(7) (B)
(8) (B)
(9) (B)
(10) (B)
(11) (B)
(12) (C)
(13) (B)
(14) (B)
(15) (A)
(16) (B)
(17) (A)
(18) (B)
(19) (B)
(20) (B)
(21) (B)
(22) (B)
(23) (A)
(24) (B)
(25) (B)
(26) (B)
(27) (A)
(28) (B)
(29) (B)
(30) (C)

4 Paragraph Practice

Questions 1–4 refer to the following paragraph.

Lisa is planning a new business venture focused on eco-friendly products. She aims to meet the increasing demand for sustainable alternatives by offering items that are both functional and environmentally conscious. Lisa's 1. _______ involves extensive research on market trends and consumer preferences. She understands that building a successful brand requires not only a great product but also a strong 2. _______ strategy. Her ultimate goal is to 3. _______ a positive impact on the environment while maintaining profitability. To do so, she plans to 4. _______ partnerships with like-minded organizations that share her vision for a greener future.

1.

(A) investment (B) strategy
(C) interest (D) challenge

2.

(A) marketing (B) customer
(C) financial (D) production

3.

(A) measure (B) maintain
(C) make (D) ignore

4.

(A) establish (B) avoid
(C) disrupt (D) simplify

〈Paragraph Practice Answer Key〉

(1) (B)

(2) (A)

(3) (C)

(4) (A)

5 Idiom Practice

1. Set the bar high – To establish high standards.
   "She always sets the bar high for herself in goal-setting."

2. Think big – To have ambitious or grand ideas.
   "He encouraged his team to think big with their new project."

3. Ahead of the curve – To be more advanced than others.
   "Adopting new technology keeps us ahead of the curve."

4. Raise the stakes – To increase the importance or risk.
   "Expanding into new markets has raised the stakes."

5. Test the waters – To try something out before committing.
   "Let's test the waters with a pilot project first."

6. In the pipeline – Being prepared or under development.
   "We have several exciting projects in the pipeline."

7. Play it by ear – To be flexible and adapt as needed.
   "If trends change, we'll play it by ear."

8. Crunch the numbers – To analyze financial data.
   "Before deciding, we need to crunch the numbers."

9. Break new ground – To innovate or do something original.
   "This project could break new ground in the industry."

10. Step up to the plate – To take responsibility or initiative.
    "It's time for the team to step up to the plate on this project."

❖ 저자 약력

조동인 교수

한국외국어대학교 영어과 졸업

뉴욕주립대 교육학 석사

한국외국어대학교 영문학 박사

현 인하공업전문대학 자유전공학부 교수

26. What does David believe about future trends in the industry?

(A) They are stable

(B) They change rapidly

(C) They don't matter

27. How does David respond to industry changes?

(A) By adjusting goals

(B) By ignoring them

(C) By consulting his team only

28. What's David's approach to employee involvement in goal-setting?

(A) He doesn't involve them

(B) He values their input

(C) He uses their input only for minor goals

29. Why does David use analytics in his planning?

(A) To predict the future accurately

(B) To help with precise goal-setting

(C) To avoid unnecessary meetings

30. What type of goals does David believe are essential for success?

(A) Short-term only

(B) Long-term only

(C) A mix of both immediate and future goals